I TAKE
THE ROAD
TO
EVEREST

I TAKE THE ROAD TO EVEREST

WALKING A PATH THROUGH TWO CENTURIES

PRAMILA LE HUNTE

Copyright © 2022 Pramila le Hunte

The moral right of the author has been asserted.
Apart from any fair dealing for the purposes of research or private study, or criticism or review, as permitted under the Copyright, Designs and Patents Act 1988, this publication may only be reproduced, stored or transmitted, in any form or by any means, with the prior permission in writing of the publishers, or in the case of reprographic reproduction in accordance with the terms of licences issued by the Copyright Licensing Agency. Enquiries concerning reproduction outside those terms should be sent to the publishers.

Matador
9 Priory Business Park,
Wistow Road, Kibworth Beauchamp,
Leicestershire. LE8 0RX
Tel: 0116 279 2299
Email: books@troubador.co.uk
Web: www.troubador.co.uk/matador
Twitter: @matadorbooks

ISBN 978 1800461 512

British Library Cataloguing in Publication Data.
A catalogue record for this book is available from the British Library.

Printed and bound in Great Britain by 4edge Limited
Typeset in 11pt Minion Pro by Troubador Publishing Ltd, Leicester, UK

Matador is an imprint of Troubador Publishing Ltd

To all my four beloved children and my nine beautiful grandchildren.

I pass and I stay, like the Universe – Alberto Caeiro

The lyf so short, the craft so long to lerne,
Th' assay so hard, so sharp the conquerynge,
The dredful joye alwey that slit so yerne:
Al this mene I by Love, that my felynge
Astonyeth with his wonderful werkynge

Chaucer: *The Parlement of Fowles*

PREFACE

I Take the Road to Everest. This book is a life saga, Pramila the author's own, set between two most beloved countries, India where she was raised, and England the country of her marriage to Bill Le Hunte. When Pramila asked me to write a preface for her most extraordinary memoir I felt it was somehow serendipitous as Pramila and I have become, over the years, co-grandmothers of three grandsons who are remarkable to both of us for their exuberance, their talents and because they are ours. My oldest son, Jan Golembiewski, married Pramila's youngest daughter, Bem Le Hunte, and that's where our paths crossed, at the exotic Indian wedding ceremony in Delhi. I had never been to India – I did not know what to expect. Pramila's broad-smiling, welcoming face, backed by the solid grace of her family home in Lutyen's Delhi, and her elegant, scrutinising mother, quizzing me in a slightly unnerving way about my son, to discern whether his education levels qualified him to marry her granddaughter. We quickly learn that there is ongoing tension between Pramila, the curious and rebellious spirit searching for her Everest and her mother, the elegant and conservative Mrs Lal content to rule from home.

Pramila had defied her mother, she is determined to stay with her personal ambitions which are going to take her far away from maternal control. She steeps herself in the requirements needed to get an entrance to Cambridge. And she wins her escape, drenched in sublime intimate hours spent with her great love Bill Le Hunte. Pramila's newly found love and thirst for English literature, her courage inspired by the quotes of Gandhi and Nehru, her grounding in the old wisdoms of the Baghvad Gita, give her the power and inspiration to interpret her own life, its splendours and calamities. The words of British poets fuel her language with rhetorical force.

When Pramila came to Australia, the tables were turned. No grand house, no servants padding around with trays of tea. No cooks and no chauffeurs. It was camping for all of us. And in her black Akubra, Prami looked every bit the part of the outback woman. She wanted to go everywhere and never complained about rough conditions or the old bombs (which were the standard transport in those days) as long as she had new vistas to explore. Opal mines that took her back to her exotic beginnings at her Father's Iron ore mines set in the jungles throbbing with wildlife.

In the meantime, the Prami caravan went everywhere and straddled the millennium absorbing the chiaroscuro of life, unpicking the dark and brutal sight of politics and racism. Even as a child knee high to a grass hopper she was an engaging little freedom fighter charging for India's freedom at the behest of her hero Mahatma Gandhi. Her powerful exposé of dictatorship in Africa wins international recognition at the Edinburgh Fringe festival. However, Pramila is not just an angry voice. Her passion to explore literature in a creative albeit eccentric way inspires her to release a basketful of pigeons in an open-air production of Shakespeare's '*Much Ado About Nothing*' to celebrate the boys home coming after the war to celebrate peace. No dove's available, pigeon was the best option! The Pramila I met was fun. A sudden challenge attacks the sweet indulgent life of self-exploration, the shockwaves of pregnancy and she starts peering into the tangle of family relationship she has experienced first-hand. The child becomes a woman, mother of four and her voice changes but the guiding star does not. A latter-day Gandhi emerges in her final published play called *Passenger* with a message where two words speak a million, "Kill no birds".

Pramila and I have had an enjoyable time cruising in tandem, through the event-filled life of our families. But Covid and advancing age has stopped our common escapades. Pramila has travelled through her own unfolding drama of teacher and politician and bears witness to its sweetness, trials and triumphs and its terrible feelings when her marriage so fundamental to her stability and self-confidence starts to fall apart. Like Humpty Dumpty who's fate always moved the young Pramila she cannot put the pieces together again. So be it. There is still the future. She hands over her mantle of green to her four children, Arjun the first born and the twin girls, Anju and Ashi and Abha who they call Bem and to her nine grandchildren and all those who embrace the amazing diversity of the beautiful world she explored.

Anybody who reads this book will be impressed by the cohort of Dickensian characters who inhabit the pages and the journey of the brave and adventurous woman who tells their tale.

Kathy Golski Author
Watched by Ancestors 1998
My Two Husbands 2008

80 Today!

Blow out those candles, Prami; your army is marking time. Reveille the troops, start the day! While you gaze at your navel, Everest awaits. Time to present your Colours to the regiment and dig in to that pièce de resistance that is your life.

Of course, I'll cut the cake, dear reader, and you'll see what tumbles out: the hooker, the baker, the chai garam maker, not to mention the curious collection of liquorice allsorts! If you hang around till eighty, you attract a bundle of camp followers now recruited into granny's army. I trust them to get me safely to Everest, entertaining you all the way through two different centuries in scenes two world but then I'm a theatre director and can bang it all together, so come along and enjoy the show and see how the plot unfurls. I know you can't drop a plumbline from Everest to my snowy hair in one steady throw, but you can still make it by the hopscotch route, springing from leaf to leaf like a frog.

> '*Sometimes you gwyne to git hurt, en sometimes you gwyne to git sick; but every time you's gwyne well again.*'
> Mark Twain: *Huckleberry Finn*.

With the odds in my favour, I'll take a chance. With a generous dose of hutzpah boosting my walking sticks, I'm like Tillie the frog bouncing all the way for a peak-to-peak tryst with my love.

The sun shone and the clouds cleared and Everest gleamed.

'Hello, my Everest! I'm Prami. At last, we've met.'

*

It was 29 May 1953 when a switched-off pupil doodling at the back of the class heard that Tiger Tenzing had conquered Everest; a mountain so out of reach even to hardened climbers, yet it surrendered to a humble Indian Sherpa. While mulling over his epic achievement, a thought took shape; first as a hint then a glint and then it fired. If a Sherpa can do it, why not me? Female though I be, I carry enough baggage for the privilege of being born a girl-child in a country that prefers sons. The destiny of an Indian girl of my time is to submit meekly an arranged marriage. It may suit some of my peers as a handy escape, but compliance to parental demand can never be my mantra. I'll find my own man, make my own life, keep moving as I forge my own way; come what may.

1938

India

A girl child is born in the cusp of history on an ambivalent see-saw of time. A pacifist saint on one end, a demon killer on the other. Gandhiji teaching non-violence, Hitler planning to annihilate Jews. It was 1938, three months before Kristallnacht, a pacifist saint on one side, a demon killer on the other. Politics hadn't really crossed my mind, though others around spoke of nothing else... the exit of the British. Yet despite their pugnacity, the anger, I was a happy child of the times though I never thought of myself as a child; I was a person and it was a beautiful planet where I first drew breath.

My parents lived in a copper mining basin of Mosaboni in eastern India that was managed by a British company from Calcutta, who in turn followed a colonial blueprint for their staff, designed in London! As simple as that: white people lived with their families in large

verandahed bungalows with tennis courts and swimming pool, and of course the Club that happened to be next to our house where come Christmas time, I was allowed to watch movies of cowboys and Indians that hoofed my hair into galloping goose bumps.

Oh, I wish I had my own horse. What fun it would be to whoop like an Indian on the warpath, bursting into the bar with an attitude cigar, creating mayhem and then gallop away into the sunset! But the galloping girl was swiftly removed from the scene by Christmas father. It was meant to be a Christmas party for the kids, totally out of order to convert it into an Indian bazaar. I tried to stand my ground; how was it possible to play cowboys and Indians without an Indian? The innocent girl did not understand that clubs are apartheid premises built by the British to keep them well insulated from the natives, and allow them a sweet taste of home. How sweet is their home? A ration of 8 oz. of sugar and preserves every two months. Yet they yearn for the sunken belly of post-war Britain.

Mother feels superior to them in every way, but I've always wondered on whose side she really belonged. I used to play with their children in the tennis courts and thought of them as friends, but Mother had warned me clearly,

'You can only regard them as acquaintances; they can never be your friends.'

Very true for we were the only Indian family living within the British community. Having us as neighbours must have been the last thing they wanted. As a result, I became the fortunate beneficiary of an *ad hoc* multicultural world.

Despite her protestations against the British, she's a legatee of an Irish convent and likes its ways, the education it provides and speaks better English than Hindi. Perhaps, she also feels superior to her husband, for he speaks English in hanging sentences. As the latest thought enters his mind, another takes over, ending up in fragmented conversation. I notice Father speaks with a stronger Indian accent, but he speaks it fluently. In her superior isolation from the British, Mother does not realise that it is Hindi that will be the language of tomorrow, especially with Independence around the corner and Mountbatten on the way.

Before he moved into mining iron ore, Father started his working life logging in forests where elephants and panthers roamed. A pioneer in solar topi, he tramped the jungles unafraid, using bullock carts to transfer the *sal* logs that he felled to Mosaboni's copper mines, set within the homeland of the Santhal tribal people with their mesmerising culture of songs and dances. He gave me a childhood to remember.

He was a slender man always dressed in cotton khaki shorts and bush shirt, light brown skin, with tortoise shell glasses, a man who felt more comfortable outdoors. He walked with a slightly clumsy gait while his wife, shall we say, 'sailed'. I recall him rumbling home with loaded bullock carts of timber from his trees, and I knew for sure that on the back of bullock carts the wild west was won, and Father I recognised as John Wayne for they regularly showed popular westerns at the British club.

As I start taking full measure of the amalgam in his mind, I recognise it in myself when I get older. I'm much closer to my father but I see much more of my mother. Difficult to lose her. Like the North star she keeps an unwavering eye on me.

As an only child, I dared my own mythology, secretly, silently lest parents catch up. It's all about them. My

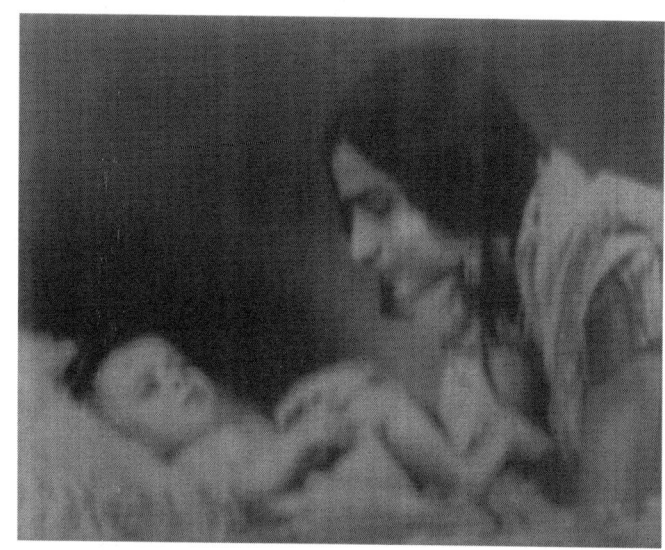

father's name is Shiv the Natraj, meaning Lord of the Dance, creator and destroyer of the universe. He holds no fear; mighty name simple dad. I can dance with him but not with the moon, Chandrakala, my mother. She is able to do both, not with the universe but with one of her own making, little Prami. She considers herself my health czar whom she nurtures like a hot house plant.

She may carry a celestial name, but mind you, she's just as capricious as her namesake, rotating from glory to gloom. When you are in her good books and study properly, you may get a 'sometime smile', more often the regulation frown that she proclaims shows her genetic, intellectual forehead! To let you into a secret, it's all put on to impress Father; I know she never goes anywhere near a proper book, she relies on the dictionary and Father is content with his Readers Digest. I'm sure, he's able to overlook that frown, for like the moon, she's just as beautiful, with classic contours that will never age. A square jawline, like Audrey Hepburn, with hair tightly pulled back, ending in a shell-shaped bun, gracefully positioned at the nape of her neck.

Victorian lady to the hilt, she somehow, begot this stowaway daughter, the wild challenge of her life. I turned out a rebel with a good cause: endless lessons and punishment if you resist. Put your head round this one; she's teaching a poem; you may not be able to see the intellectual forehead, but you can certainly hear the frown.

> *'A beetle got stuck in some jam*
> *And he cried,*
> *'Oh, how unhappy I am.'*

And his Ma said,
'Don't talk, if you really can't walk,
"You'd better go home in a tram.'
Anon

Her compulsion drove her, drove me, to mountains of excellence. My education has become Mother's Magnificent Obsession.

I may sound erudite, but I'm not; just Mother's dictionary coming out. I have a penchant for words I half-understand; they roll round the tongue like music, yet I would not be where I am without that little yellow book, *The Songs the Letters Sing*.

What more can a dictionary sing from its verbal generosity? The tune of my life. Let us begin. The tram is on it's way.

My Childhood in India

'Yesterday is gone, tomorrow has not yet come.
We have only today, let us begin.'
Mother Teresa

Living life backwards to childhood in India, innocent memories sweeten with time. Our long verandah in Mosaboni where the show is frisky; cavorting, tumbling and shrieking with the ever-ever swinging skipping rope. Life itself is so much joy, sticky with the juice of mangoes dripping from the corner of the mouth and leaking out to an orange slosh-spladge on my *dhobi*-cleaned pillow. I was a happy child, tucked away in a little nowhere.

Night-time I sleep alone with Hari ayah for company, but that doesn't count because she snores throughout and that gives me time to create my own special world. Here there is no Mickey Mouse, Bugs Bunny or Chicken Little; I had real nursery around me. Busy Micky was an active little scooper when village women threshed rice after harvest, and bunnies came out in the field in numbers with no village dogs to give chase, and instead of Chicken Little, the *junglee* fowl scampered about the wilderness, dawn and dusk. What beauties! They are the whipper-snipper of dawn, greeting the day with colour and cackling. Wait for night and the secret porcupine crosses the road, watched by ever-present sentinel, the nightjar waiting always on the dusty dirt road. What is hidden behind the sal trees is larger than life; elephant families, whose every movement thrashes the trees.

I wake up suddenly to the peacock's morning scream. I'm not in the trees like Tarzan and his Cheetah, but in my lovely white-washed, talcum powder bungalow, where a peacock lurks outside. Sworn enemy of cook, attacking him fiercely as he runs the dangerous corridor between cook house and bungalow to get my breakfast. Why so angry with the cook and so friendly with the butler? It was really the cook who gave him the grain!

Morning has begun as usual; breakfast will be on the table. Time to play with Onesta Sylvestri, my Italian friend who has just arrived. For, me the past is play and performance. What a little actress I was even then, although a little madam. Thought myself a poet of consequence! Every room has a memory, the most of the verandah where I spend hours with an Italian girl.

> I have a friend and we play.
> A little blue China teapot and tea.
> Onesta Sylvestri and me
> It's children's tea party on the verandah
> When parents are away.
> We hold tiny, blue cups

        and try to sip like ladies
        like mummy does.
    We make little slurp, slurp noises,
  'Too hot' says Onesta. Let me wait.'
  'No. finish it.' I put on Mummy's voice.
        She rises to leave.
    'Why should I drink your real tea?
It's bitter. And what my ayah makes is sweet.'

We skipped away for a year and a day, not minding the heat of the sun. I pause for breath, and Onesta has gone. She's in prison because she's Italian, and Italians are sent to prison, for there's a war going on; something to do with Hitler and Lord Haw-Haw on the radio. He rings a bell 'ting-ting-ting', to announce British ships going down. Father tells me, he's a traitor, but for me, I enjoy his name. It's strange to enjoy the war for little things.

So, life goes on in the bungalow. Nothing much to report except there was a dog, called Tojo; Mother shooed Tojo away; Uncle shot a python on our tree. Perhaps, he was after Tojo. We don't want Japanese here. Uncle calls him canine *non grata*. Like Italians he's an enemy; it's all so confusing, this fighting stuff.

I'm bored to tears with Hari ayah for company; I'm allowed to do nothing for myself. One evening I take the initiative. I decide to climb the guava tree of the python. You can peer over the wall to the English club from where I heard giggles coming from the garden at night. Naughty, naughty! I'm growing up; I know about such things. It's not Christopher Robin saying his prayers. Hari ayah catches the knowing smile on my face and quickly pulls me down.

'Baby, these things are not for you.'

I don't want to be Baby anymore! I want to grow up and not be tied down to English lessons. There's a world outside.

If wishes were horses, Prami will ride. Shyama gave me my first taste of the real world when on a bright Wednesday morning my pony bolted; she flew like Pegasus with a curly-topped adventurer on her back.

1946

On the road to Everest on a pony

Father has gifted me a lovely pony after relentless pleadings. It was not really gifted; she was the product of pester- power knowing that Father is the only parent who would relent.

Shyama is a quiet, brown pony with something resembling a white star smudged on her forehead, rather in the way a priest would rub a *tilak* of amber paste on mine after a religious *puja*. She releases me from the bungalow and I take little rides in the morning, with my *sais,* the groom, just the usual ramble, past the only church on the left, the only grocery store on the right; both go unnoticed as neither has much to offer. Essentials have to come from Calcutta like best imported olive oil for my ringlets.

The start of this daily excursion is nothing extraordinary; we move along the macadamised rise housing Anglo-Indian bungalows; they don't live near the *burra sahibs* for they are mixed breed, half-baked bread as Mother calls them, aping the British, thinking less of the Indians. Best keep them in their place.

We amble past the tennis court cages protected by black curtains from the sun on all sides and follow the dirt-track straight onto the tribal Santhal village, where my *sais*, who is also a Santhal, finds welcome. It's endless fun, playing with wooden shavings that lie scattered around like butterflies in the dust blown off from timber-laden Bedford trucks coming from the forests that surround Mosaboni.

Mother has never even guessed that I play these *junglee* games. Had she got wind of these pleasure-breaks on the dirt-track, a bombshell would explode over the intellectual forehead.

She calls these people, *junglees*, not as name-calling, but in normal conversation as: 'I use *junglee malis* in my garden; *junglee* servants are so unreliable. You give them money on Tuesday to spend at the weekly Wednesday market, and you don't see them for the rest of the week.'

Well, today happens to be Wednesday morning and I can hear Mother bossing the servants. I shall have sneak peek at forbidden territory. I call out to the *sais* and he lifts me on the pony.

Today, something's wrong, for the pony's saddle feels loose. Very slowly it begins to shift, slipping along the neck like a cautious tortoise, one careful jolt at a time, in unison with the bullock cart ruts ridging the road. I call out to the *sais*, '*Dekho*', look, what's happening!' Before he can do anything, the pony makes her own decision. She bolts, and within seconds the racing sais becomes a speck, waving arms frantically. I dare not look back for one slight movement will have me toppled. I am in serious trouble; the saddle might easily tip sideways or go catapulting over the pony's head! I tell myself John Wayne didn't ever fall off; neither will you!

I hang on with all my might to whatever I can find along her sweaty neck. I notice long black hairs underneath the saddle. Probably her mane. I clutch it in desperation; there's no way anyone can reach me. To my amazement I remain on top, feeling anything but heroic. Past the lime green paddy fields the pony gallops into villagers setting off for the weekly market, or *haat* as it's called.

Women with baskets of produce, balanced regally on their heads, step aside and survive; men with two baskets dangling from a pole on their shoulders, first wobble, then tumble. Little black pigs tied to poles squealing upside down, crescendo their shrieking; chickens held firmly upside down accept defeat.

We veer round a bullock cart, avoiding head-to-head collision. All is chaos and confusion. Eventually, we reach the Santhal village; a young boy playing on the road, chasing a bicycle wheel without spokes, leaps onto the desperate pony, and with lightning swiftness, holds the reigns.

The whole village has gathered with curiosity; they disperse at the horn of the racing jeep. It's Father in solar topi and khaki shorts who has been alerted about the disaster. Jumping off the jeep he grabs me high and flings me on the seat: I remember a girl howling with curls amuck, red dirt on her face.

I don't recollect much else except that he rewards the boy handsomely. All the village pats him as a hero. I'm very upset because it's me who's really is the hero, the stout adventurer who has so bravely fought the monsters and survived! I had to make an issue of neglect but Father has spotted the sulk, but taking no notice, guides me through the market, now in full display.

The women spread their produce on the ground, and balance babies on slings as they bargain over okra, bitter gourd, packs of dried chillies or basketful of custard apples. Behind their back no shortage of live food for the table, pigs-n-all.

Men gather at the home-made liquor stall. Naturally, the *haat* is their club. No festival in these arid regions of India can do without cockfight and toddy. A group of men, eyes red and swollen with booze, form a ring where the birds' legs are being strapped with sharp blades, and prominent among them a curly-haired man was pushing the villagers to convert the usual cockfight into a confrontation of a white cock against a multi-plumed one. Father told me he's was the school master. The Colosseum of the Indies is preparing for a festival.

The wide world was opened when my pony bolted; I was pitchforked headlong into a world that I could never have seen and a man I'd never known.

The pony ride had revealed an entirely different man. He had spent time with me without the interface of Mother. In the Wednesday market I noticed he appeared well known and liked by the supposed '*junglees*'; the headmaster was his friend. I was beginning to imagine the other side of this extraordinary man who begot me; that would have to wait for Father is shoving me through the chaos to the curly-haired man I had noticed in the melee.

He turned out to be the headmaster of the local missionary school. And surprisingly, a friend of Father. I feel ill at ease in his presence; I've seen him instigating the cockfight. Hero or villain? He was being treated as a VIP with all the participating cocks being brought over to him for inspection.

Our introduction is quite informal, a hug and a *namaste*. 'This is Principal of the village school, known as Michael Sir to all,' and 'this' pointing at me, 'is my daughter, Prami, the little heroine you might have seen galloping like a princess on her pony.' I'm glad he called me 'heroine' at last!

I hold out my hand, he nods and looks away. Perhaps one shouldn't touch princesses. Maybe I look nothing like a princess. The prevailing wind from country liquor has made my stomach turn and the dramatic pony ride has driven my hair askew. A witch would be more appropriate.

Michael is clearly a Santhal, yet he's dressed in greyish shirt and brownish trousers with a hanging tie, looking very casual British. I couldn't stop staring at him, till I can't hold the silence any longer and continue in the politest of ways.

'I'm very happy to talk to a Santhal who can speak good English, Sir,' I say, oozing smile and confidence.

Father kicks me in the shin; Michael is acid in his reply.

'I shall accept your arcane flattery with the contempt it deserves.'

I have jumped in feet first. I naturally associated Santhals as domestic staff. How ignorant can one be? His English was better than mine. I had to rectify this insult; I sugared my *faux pas* like an icing on a cake that I had neither baked nor iced.

'You must be very learned.' I flatter, hoping for a grown-up chat, when a volley of screams comes from the arena. Instantly, I cover my ears.

Michael tries to calm me down.

'It's merely a festival, miss; no festival of ours is without rice beer and all-night dancing.' He turns to Father. 'The game, rugby that some of the *sahibs* play, is really hyped-up tribal warfare with heavy intake of beer and shouting on both sides, not so different from this cockfight that you are shortly to witness.'

I knew about the outcome of such events from the servant's gossip. It made me cry out,

'But I don't want to witness any of it!'

Michael seems to take no offence. I'm pulling Father away when I come to a sudden halt. I can already hear the drums and perk up at the thought of watching all-night dancing.

'Is the dancing far from here?

'In the next village' he replies.

That's sufficiently close for me to make the next move.

'I want to see this all-night dancing.'

Like ladies, it's also child's privilege to change her mind.

'It's better you go home, miss,' says Michael. 'The fight is about to start. What you'll see will be even more noisy, and not fit for your delicate ears'.

He's trying to talk down to me and I don't like it at all; Father is pulling me away at the same time.

'I'll bring Prami over to you another time,' he says, 'then she can play with the village children.'

God be with him if Mother gets to know. I stand my ground with baleful arms akimbo; I will not budge. Talk about being independent! Father makes a deal, 'Ten minutes only.' He holds me fast.

Thump-thump was picking up in the darkness beyond.

*

I arrive back home late, my clothes smelling of toddy, and guess who is waiting? The veritable moonbeam. Her face darkens, there's an eclipse in offing. Not a chance of that 'sometime' smile.

'Straight to bed!' She orders. 'Your lessons will start the first thing tomorrow.'

They are having a right old ding-dong as I leave. Couldn't help thinking how did he marry such a superior wife? Now here is a man who has made good on his own. and he's done it the hard way, on foot.

I remember clearly the hubbub of a search party being mustered to search areas where he had been prospecting. He could well be lying beneath some tree with malaria or a broken-down jeep, or even worse, a victim of animal attack. Lucky, they found him alive. As Father rose in life, pressure was put on to find a wife to share with him the wilderness that was now his home. This man is a steeplechaser, a jumper of obstacles; he must now jump the last hurdle.

Interrogation! Imagine him consulting a future father-law.

Question:	What job are you in?
Answer:	Mining.
Question:	What are you mining, gold?
Answer:	I'm afraid not. Only iron ore.
Question:	How can you dress my daughter in iron ore?
Answer:	There is very little gold mined in India, but heaps of iron ore.
Question:	How awfully metallic!
Answer:	So is iron ore.

Touché, Daddy. My grandfather might be looking for gold, but finds his comeuppance in the Rock of Ages. Everything was going to plan. Father was already thirty years old and prepared to marry a lady he did not know.

It took Father over thirty years to scale this mountain, Mother did it in one. I don't mean one year, one month or even just a day.

In fact, Mother did it with a single word. She didn't huff, most certainly, she didn't puff; she was modest.

It would be unseemly in those days to come out with a bold, 'Yes', lest it implied: 'Yes, I fancy that man', She just *Humphed*. Mother was established for life as a woman of status just with that little grunt. Little cry, but, so much wool. Never underestimate the power of 'Hmmph!' It made her life, and also made me.

I'm the offspring of 'Hmmph'.

1946

Mosaboni: War and Peace

'I want to see Freedom immediately, this night before dawn, it can be had... Here is a mantra, a short one that I give... The mantra is "Do or Die" ... We shall not live to see the perpetuation of our slavery.'
Gandhi Speech, 1942

A sepia image emerges out from time: I'm eight and a half years old. The child Mother modelled so painstakingly with cute ringlets has morphed into an unruly freedom fighter. I see myself lurching forward in a tennis court to hurl a stone at my white playmate. Sure, there's justification behind this.

Parents are always glued to the radio; sometimes I sit with them and breathe inspiration like a whiff of gunpowder. I actually heard Gandhiji on the radio. It was his cry to action, to 'Do or Die'. I'm not quite sure what he's saying, but the adrenalin in his voice is enough to get me going, to hurl a cushion sailing across the carpet. Not Gandhian, I'm afraid. He's for *ahimsa*, non-violence; I like violent stuff. Naturally, I get spanked.

'This child must be tamed, brought in line,' declares Mother.

No effect on me. That same afternoon I'm determined to try it out. I approach my usual playmate, Margaret, step by step, eye to eye, a little stone in my hand.

'Quit India!' I challenge and hurl the little stone. That now makes me officially a freedom fighter!

We may be playmates but all is fair in love and war. I have to become a resolute warrior and follow Gandhiji. Margaret turns around and does the same. India and Britain are now at war.

Both our ayahs gossiping nearby clutch their saris to their blouses, aghast at my sudden volley. I have attacked the mines superintendent's daughter!

The moment Hari ayah finds my forehead bleeding, she rushes me home to Mother. The rest is high drama.

'Where's the girl's mother?' An angry voice getting louder and louder, more and more furious, has already entered the mine superintendent's house, with a distraught security guard trying his best to restrain this lady's march forward. He can't really apprehend a lady of her status. She is well known as S. Lal's' powerful wife.

'Call the girl's mother. Quickly, quickly', she commands, 'You, over there, don't hang about, *jaldi, jaldi!*'

Her voice is his command. The man scurries to fetch the master, leaving behind a lady throwing cow dung, right, left and centre at the British.

Had I broken the rhythm of her retribution; the cow dung might well have landed on my face. I hold my silence till Mr Herbert, the mines superintendent comes out with Margaret following closely behind; a smug little miss, to say the least.

'Your daughter has thrown a stone at my child in the tennis court and made a hole in her forehead,' shrills the lady, pointing at my bloodied bandage.

Naturally, the hullabaloo brings out the lady of the house. Her husband greets the woman politely, carefully keeping his distance. You can't shake hands with dynamite.

'I'll ask my daughter to come forward immediately and apologise.' He indicates to his wife to bring the little criminal to dock.

Margaret stands her ground.

'Your whole damn country and your king need to apologise,' shrills the parent. 'Why don't you get the silly man to stammer his apologies.'

'Now, now, Madam, let's be calm. We'll get to the bottom of this.' He takes a step forward this time. 'In no way will I allow my daughter to get away with this brutish behaviour.'

'Don't they say in your Bible, turn the other cheek? Well, do so now!'

Mother bends down purposefully, pulls off her sandal, and makes out as if she would smash it into his face. I was taken by surprise wondering if Gandhiji's movement was suddenly getting violent. I had been smacked earlier for just throwing a mere cushion and now this, a sandal on the face? Hurrah for her, for once.

The altercation on the front verandah has excited her entire staff. The *mali* quickly puts his gardening shears down, tucks his dhoti tightly round him so that it would not flap, and peeped from behind the high-rise orange canna beds; the *gwala*, bringing his well-washed cow for supervised milking by the *memsahib,* is startled in the back drive when curiosity rushes him forward, leaving his cow untethered. Inside, the bearer quietly opens a window where he's supposedly polishing silverware. The sweepress sits on her haunches at the other end of the verandah, and prays for invisibility. The entire domestic staff is agog; never have they seen a white man attacked by an Indian woman.

'Quit India!' I repeat, raising my arm and going for her.

On the field, the cavalry charges.

'You're doing it again, you stupid Indian. You get out!'

Margaret is about to hurl her violin when Mrs Herbert puts her ample form round each shoulder. Turning to Mother, she manages a smile.

'Can I take you inside, lady, for a nice cup of tea?' She holds out her hand even as a white flash and thrashing horns behind the bougainvillea announce that the cow has gone amuck. Without a second thought, shrieking and giggling, the two of us chase after the *gwala* as he desperately tries to disentangle the horns of his bovine source of bread.

'To the cowshed, my bewties,' commands the *memsahib*, 'I should've kept you there, or even milked you myself. Whoa, whoa, get away!'

All hostility blown over, Margaret and I follow the bovine in question, back to her lawful residence.

Meanwhile, her husband is quick to usher his erstwhile sparring partner into the drawing room where he waits on her with old-world courtesy. He pulls up a high-backed upholstered chair and tries to seat her as she struggles. It's difficult to put a ramrod in a sitting position.

'You don't want to get your clothes torn, Ma'am. I'll bring your daughter back straight away.'

Just at that moment the two of us arrive hand in hand, challenging each other as to who got hold of the tail first!

'You both did it well,' placates the lady of the house. She's dishevelled and panting, with one of her earphone plaits unravelling down and her blue chrysanthemum dress in disarray.

'You both won! Bethany is back in the shed, God bless her.' She turns to her husband,

'Look! Both children are chattering, boiling like pea soup.' She has to raise her voice to be heard.

'What's your name, nipper?'

'Prami, from the tennis court.'

'Beautiful, Prami, I'll take you to the cowshed, and show you how to milk the cow.'

As I look at Mother, pleading with my eyes, the aristocratic nose quivers in wrath.

'I'm not letting you go anywhere with that girl', concludes Mother, hands firmly on my shoulder.

'With your kind permission, Ma'am, would you graciously allow your daughter to stay back.'

Mr Herbert is charm itself, and slowly melts the angry

lady who realises that her staff would see me returning home escorted by the chauffer of the big boss.

I got to know later he was breaking rules, for his company had warned him,

'Mixing with Indians can only lead to trouble. You're doing well with us. Do you want Gandhi and his mob at your doorstep, old chap?'

'Yes', Aunty had said, she would have liked to have opened the door to the dhoti, even given him a cup of tea!

Lovely lady.

Happily, I became a fly on the wall and thought of Aunty as a second mother. There's an unseen bond between us. She listens to my domestic woes and I was able to dry her tears when Margaret was sent to a boarding school in Wales.

I hope to meet them one day in her precious country for Uncle Herbert has got just a few months left of his tour.

Meanwhile, my own little sojourn in Mosaboni must end. Father's business has so expanded that he must set up head office in Calcutta. I'm told good schools await me, but I don't want to leave my Mosaboni.

1947

Off we go, Calcutta 'Hello'

Alarmed, portentous rumours are about, like Chinese whispers, fearfully hushed.

'*Sahib* is leaving! *Sahib* is leaving, *sahib* is leaving!'

The ground is moving! Rumours fly and multiply: *Sahib's* garage would close, unstocking with one motion, the coterie of self-promoted quartermasters in our workshop, sitting on lucrative, back-hander jobs!

Serves them right! I don't like those fellows with large bellies protruding from vests stopping just short by the navel, and betel juice dripping down from the side of their mouths. They spit the red juice against the whitewashed garage wall. Disgusting!

In some quarters, like with our '*junglee*' staff, there is joy. *Memsahib* wouldn't persecute *mali* anymore for his ineptitude as a gardener, his failure as a foot soldier to load her armoury with those gigantic, green spears of okra that made her triumphant, gave her the power that she needed, and I feared; white stinging hairs, retaliatory when touched, lances of apprehension. She has always regarded herself the garden's quartermaster.

My reverie of garden warfare is interrupted. A car horn is pumping impatiently; the cook standing beside is trying to *salaam* while dodging our violent peacock; will they ever make friends? A second horn signals trouble; Hari ayah is looking for me! Calcutta calls!

I shall hide in *mali's* vegetable garden, and I'll give you my final thoughts from the bushes.

Do we really want to go to Calcutta? I had asked this question before. Here's the triumvirate answer:

Mother: affirmative; it would allow her to live like a lady, more comfort, modern sanitation 'that means' no smelly thunder-boxes, emptied daily by a low-caste sweeper. I'm sure the lady feels she has been brought down in life. To be honest, arranged marriage is nothing short of a gamble.

Instead, she hopes to find there will be fine stores and trips to fruit markets for her 'work', for that's what she calls her little sorties for bargaining.

Father: probably; he was pulled two ways. As his business expands, he needs civilisation; end to stand and shout business conversations into a telephone fixed too high on the wall. Time for a modern head office in Calcutta and a mines office in the growing township of Barbil. He tries to persuade me but he has never been successful with a recalcitrant daughter.

Baby: very categorically, '*Never*'! The wilderness still calls.

How far is this true? Now this wild 'thing' that I craved for, was it magical as the tree-hidden home of

Tarzan and Cheetah, with elephants on call? No, it was born of my imagination. To tell you the truth, with the exception of a few treasured moments, I seldom left Mosaboni, yet something, somewhere, among rushing rivers and sunlight-shielded jungles, illumines a place called 'Freedom'. For that I must search. It will never be in Calcutta.

'Baby, Baby, Baby, where are you?' I hear someone thrashing the undergrowth. If I duck, they will not see me, my heart is pounding!

The ground beneath me trembles and shifts, a seismic warning? Snakes are holding the Earth, says the legend; when one of them moves, earthquakes happen, but there were no crows taking off in confusion as when earthquakes happen; they crackled the dawn, as usual, CAW, CAW, CAW, forgetting the strike of monsoon lightning that... chose, one of their homes on the jasmine tree, and gave Mother an excuse for felling the rest, too near the house, too high. They were already familiar with the thud-thud of miners blasting rocks below our house, but not that their own would be blasted.

'At last, I've got you!' Hari ayah has found me and is pulling my ear in frustration. It has taken a long time unearthing me from my alternative universe.

As we leave Mosaboni, fully packed, I take a last look at my past: This is the road of my pony ride where me and Shyama trod. It's a memory of sadness that I never rode Shyama again. I feel now that Father should have pushed me to ride her. If you give up so easily you will never ride. Those are the tennis courts on the crossroads where I fought for my country, and beyond is the village where the Santhals danced. I'm now leaving the house of Aunty Herbert, but she has left it a while ago to retire in Wales. One day we shall all meet.

When the travel bug bites there will be no relenting. As I'm about to cut the first slice, the first chapter of my life, I can see a little girl on the wings of the peacock. May I have his tenacity of purpose. What will the poor sod do when there is no cook to fight?

1947-1957

Calcutta

'We shape our dwellings and afterwards our dwellings shape us.'
Eric Nebel: Quote from Winston Churchill

'They pack em in like sardines here!' observed a white tourist on entering Calcutta.

I wondered whether this tourist was challenged by the dare of a few acres of land to contain the seed corn of humanity within its grasp. For that's what it would feel like on a rickshaw ride through this teeming city; orchestrated by the brass horns of truck drivers, the clap-clap tinkling of rickshaw bells, and the characteristic soprano of a Bengali voice, vociferously defending her pitch. The brimming population toppled off Colonial buildings, sari dangling balconies, crumbling-plaster housing, and landed where the real drama took place, the pavements of Calcutta.

A water hydrant family displays its open-plan life style by the steps of Father's Head Office, now recognised by the board, S. Lal and Co (P) Ltd. We are on a busy thoroughfare, totally unsuited for alfresco theatricals. When we parked along the adjacent pavement, we came across a naked toddler, squatting precariously over huge bouncing bubbles that both washed and tickled his unwiped behind. He burst upon the scene, nose jammed on the back window pane, pulling cute faces while his mother squatted on the pavement absorbed over a makeshift kerosene stove spreading its fumes in the air. Noxious though its fumes, deafening the horns, curiosity triggered me to pull down the window.

Within an instant, Mother roughly jerks away my hand, banshee-shrieking, 'cholera, typhoid, dysentery'! As if pulling down the glass would open Calcutta's Pandora's box. I was forbidden to touch the little boy putting out his hand, for he's a beggar. In my simplicity, I had no idea of what's a beggar and beggars are full of disease.

To Mother's horror I had already thrown out a piece of cake, and one thing led to another; we were surrounded by a horde of chattering voices that assembled from nowhere. Though I couldn't understand a word of what they said in Bengali, it was obvious they were holding out their hand for a few coins. Calcutta is a boiling cauldron of many tongues, the Babel of West Bengal. Folk arrive from all over to earn a few *paisa* for a small pot of rice soaked in just a handful of green chillies.

One woman showed a baby with an empty milk bottle and waved it in front of the car window. I was too young to take in her message of poverty and hunger. Just thought the baby looked cute. Innocence is bliss.

'Which village you come?' a beggar asked in Hindi as she peered into the taxi. I wanted to deliver a suitable riposte.

'We came on the back of an elephant.'

Unfortunately, all we had to show for stature was a black and yellow taxi. The woman continued tapped on the window as the driver started the engine.

Years later, on a holiday visit to Calcutta, my daughter-in-law comes across beggars on the road. This time with much more grotesque performers, the diseased, the deformed and the crippled; some needy, some wily, almost like professional performers.

'Puppy eyes!' she would whisper, and both children dutifully averted their gaze, or place both hands over their eyes. Could their blindness be bliss?

As the taxi speeds homewards, I reflect on the incident with recently acquired juvenile philosophy. Does poverty make people *junglees*?

The house that Father has selected for us turns out just right for the upwardly mobile, even the address is upmarket. Won't Mother relish a home in 10/1 Rowland Road, where the road itself sounds colonial; its added asset, being proximity to the Victoria Memorial a glorious building of white marble with dome, turrets and monumental gardens and fountains, a celebration of Britain's imperial past? Or was it just a failed attempt at a copycat Taj Mahal. Maybe, it's just right for the likes of her, for I'm afraid, Mother might be a fraud despite her stance against the British.

We disembarked at our 'des res'. What a glorious porch! We had certainly come up in life, no more bullock carts for Father. Our house in Calcutta reflected his rising fortunes; it was colonially impressive, columns with capitals rose Greekishly on both sides garlanded by the *mali* at Mother's direction, with arching, red bougainvillea, very similar to those I had seen at the Herbert's grand home. She must have noticed more than I had thought in her aggressive march to the mine superintendent's front door and instructed the mali in advance.

We dismount on a porch spelling colonial superiority, designed for the entry of horse and carriage. I can imagine its sleek cargo of Raj ladies in silken gowns and shawls, servants, *salaaming*, and that sort of mannered nonsense.

More than the grand front porch I prefer the backside of the building. Along the servant's quarters a huge *peepal*, the sacred fig, arises and spreads its canopy, with its bark light grey, peeling in patches; when the wind blows its leaves flutter a concert of falling rain. Directly above you'll find my room. My residency was simplicity itself, one desk, one bed, plus a cobra below. What more can I need? Some books?

Mother has decided on a convent for my education. Was this the 'good school' that was promised?

I have even been taken to meet a slow-walking lady in a starched white gown and beads dangling at her waist, who introduced herself as Mother Superior. What cheek, I thought, to elevate herself higher than the lady in soft chiffon flowing with water colour flowers, the garb that sets her up as a Greek goddess.

The lady sits down stiffly, legs together, and talks to Mother, praising their modern education. All the while she examines this specimen in front through her piercing, see-through eyes, dismembering me, exposing me for the *junglee* that I am. Not fit for any convent, I suppose. I'll give her a run for her money; I widen my thighs, lean back, and during the telling of the convent's mission statement, I let out an audible yawn. No reaction from her. With controlled discipline, she gets up from her seat and pushes my legs together. With the rebel in me rising, I make myself comfortable again, the way I was. I'm being made to feel guilty before I've done anything wrong.

Deliberately, I turn my eyes towards the black and white photographs hanging in the parlour: rows of girls sitting primly on a bench, poker-faced, even their socks follow a straight line. Mother Superior notices my gaze and the little bit of mockery at the edge of my lips. She snuffs an incoming comment as we make our departure from this this catacomb of silence.

The Escape Route

The magnum erupts the moment we reach home.

'No, I will never go to such a school.

When I had glanced at matrimonial columns in the Sunday papers, I discovered, to my horror, that a BA is considered a passport to marriage, and being convent educated an added bonus. Doesn't this parent plan so strategically in advance? She must be resisted.

So, lock up your daughter. Better still, lock me out, for I will not live in this Black Hole of Calcutta! Who has not heard of this dungeon in Fort William? Like the black carrion crows atop trees in Mosaboni, Calcutta too is riddled with left-overs of the Raj like the droppings of carrion birds. At the moment, what matters is my entombment for I had gone well beyond what songs the letters may sing or tales the letters may wish to tell. I wanted real books. They were denied to me as Mother was wary of popular reading; it would lead me up the Bollywood path, and therein lies the rub. Bogus romance in the pictures would whisk me far away from the domain of an arranged marriage.

A little chink appears in the 'Black Hole'. Father has now become a member of Calcutta's iconic Victoria Club, once the Holy Grail of the British that had finally opened its forbidden doors to the Indians. In the Great Hall, portraits of previous British presidents keep watch. Only well-to-do dared enter, and Father has made the grade.

Deep within the inner sanctum lodges its mothball library, and praise be to Victoria, she has given me access to books.

God made this mother withered and dry, till very much later, she devoured the grandchildren's Mills and Boon collection of silly romantic paperbacks. Ironic how time regresses; did these books reveal what she had missed in her salad days; did they still have the power of 'sexcitement'; was she, at last, young at heart?

My education really begins at The Victoria Club library. Father introduces me to the librarian. He's a retired army officer, a grandee with a spreading moustache, finely tuned upwards to take off like a rocket. The man was bristling with manic excitement at the prospect of a Japanese invasion. There were silver zeppelin balloons in the sky to deter Japanese planes. They had reached Burma already!

'If they dared enter our land, he'd give them a piece of his mind.' As he thumped, his moustache quivered.

Apart from his rhetoric, he was a normal gentleman who warmly welcomed me into his mothball interior and proudly paraded his leather-bound battalion. Rows and rows of stacked books, bound with peeling maroon leather, rose like a crumbling brick fortress all the way up to the high ceiling. Difficult to breathe in this place with curtains drawn and high windows that were probably too dangerous to open. One had to be careful and keep a distance from the wobbly shelves lest their contents tumble over, for his troops were octogenarians as well and probably disabled. A sliver of sunlight proved it is day, though one would hardly have believed it in a place that time had left behind. As expected, Gandhi and Nehru are fully represented, fresh marigolds were placed in front in front of each. I stopped and bowed to each of them, quietly sending a message.

Suddenly, my reverie was shattered by a blast of thunder coming from a stool.

> *"Sir, if the British Government imagines it can continue to exploit them and play about them against their will, as it has done for so long in the past, then it is grievously mistaken. It has misjudged their present temper and read history in vain."*

Nehru speech from Gorakhpur trial 1922
The librarian is reading aloud from a book with power and passion. Jawaharlal Nehru had thrown down the gauntlet.

'What happened after that?' I enquired.

'He got four years of rigorous imprisonment.' I fell silent. Now here's man without fear who would dare Everest. If I try oratory like that, I'd come out a pipsqueak. but I have a collected a battalion of words that I can deploy as silver bullets when put pen to paper for Punditji, I'm a freedom fighter just like you. I started pulling out more tomes on Nehru. The librarian was at my side, putting them back.

'Why don't you try some children's books?' he suggested and took me to *Alice in Wonderland* but it didn't interest me at all. I know that girl and her la-di-dah ways, but it was *Alice through and Looking Glass* that changed my view. I took it home and there was Humpty Dumpty sitting on the wall legs crossed like a Turk I couldn't help but think of Mother sitting cross-legged at the head of the table picking holes in the egg that has split open, monarch of her kitchen.

> *'The question is,' said Humpty Dumpty, 'which is to be master – that's all.'*
> Lewis Carroll: *Through the Looking Glass*

Simple as that; it's not going to be Mother. Out with her poems and her verbs; Humpty Dumpty will become my new guru.

> *'When I use a word,' Humpty Dumpty said, in rather a scornful tone, 'it means just what I choose it to mean – neither more nor less.'*
> Ibid

I'm a dictionaryholic as it is; Humpty made me a writer. I could create words, like g*uruship*, and *malego* for his male ego. It is he who is the *primum-mobile* of my mastery of words.

'*Salaam* to you, Humpty Dumpty! I leave you sitting on a wall as I relish my cake.

Please do not topple with the times. My memory of you is quintessential. I have spent much of my life as an educator and it started with you and with the confidence you gave me.

We touch the feet of gurus in India, but respected egg, you have no feet.' So *namaste* guru ji, I take your leave and march on.

And thus, my growing years became a bookstall of the mind, and all because of a vociferous moustache with a passion for history and pride in his country who unwittingly became my captive and granted me the right to borrow whatever I enjoyed.

I took a shine to Marianne Dashwood in *Sense and Sensibility* by Jane Austen. She's the impulsive one, the reckless one, always impassioned and uncontrolled; she loves with a warmth that leaps over all barriers, even barriers of propriety. Like a conqueror with priceless booty, I hoarded my treasure safely atop a toilet with a high, old-fashioned cistern. I could shimmy up with ease, but it's something a genteel lady like Mother wouldn't even try!

I became an adolescent partaking in the easy currency of Toilet and Torch, growing up secretly beneath bedcovers that added more pieces of eight than a school could ever provide.

How many nuns equal fun?

*'You still remember and hum some of your school
hymns and Christmas carols; Moral Science was more
important than actual science; Sex education class
bottom-line: Sex before marriage = Impurity = Sin;
Indian festival holidays + Catholic holidays = Amazing
School Life.'*
Sangeeta Sarma: Story pick, 6th April 2014

In my new school, I have turned turtle since my first contact with the Mother Superior. I had expected regimented girls I had noticed in the photographs on her wall.

Mother Superior had praised her institution as being very modern, so modern that we are expected to speak Queen's English at a school, promoted by Irish nuns in a country awaiting independence from the Brit!

In a county brimming with patriotic zeal, our history teachers went to William and Mary and the British need of Protestant monarchs and unsurprisingly, the issues to hand were promulgated by Catholic nuns! They would never take in the bizarity of my observation for the Irish have a little history of their own; their 'troubles' in a country divided by religion. Yet, it is one individual who binds them, St. Patrick, the patron saint of Ireland.

On Paddy's Day we celebrated his feast and the hall resounded with 'Hail Glorious Saint Patrick, dear Saint of our Isle' and asked him to bestow his sweet smile on Bengali children who he might have missed. If willing he could also pay his respects to my Anglo-Indian friends because they are Catholic. We ended the day with a girlie 'social'.

Mother blamed the nuns for introducing western entertainment.

'It's what Anglo-Indians do. Not us.'

'Half baked bread', she calls them. They are perfectly normal people, cooked to a turn under the Indian sun.

She's seen enough of the English at Mosaboni, and whatever she saw of Western culture she despised, for

these Anglo-Indians tried to ape the British. Certainly not with their food, Mother: breast bone pepper water, chicken country captain, and no-bake carpet pudding. Could a British chef ever produce these extraordinary names? The departing conquerors left behind their legacy, the undaunted chicken country captain who reported for duty in their tiffin box.

I owe a debt to my school; it was there that I found my love of poetry. I can still hear my beloved Mother Damien in an English class, her soft Irish voice making magic of sensuous beauty.

> *'Full on this casement shone the wintry moon,*
> *And threw warm gules on Madeline's fair breast,*
> *As down she knelt for heaven's grace and boon;*
> *Rose-bloom fell on her hands, together prest.'*
> Keats: *The Eve of St. Agnes*

She conveys to us nubile schoolgirls the throb of passion. Even though she's a nun, yet she's still a woman, for she is the bride of Christ who on her wedding day must have felt the stirrings of young love.

Shucks to Mother who sees convent education merely as an entrée to marriage. Amongst the nuns there are many who devote their lives to a foreign land.

They would hardly like to be seen as go-betweens in the marriage market, but simply as workers of Jesus.

> *'He has told us that He is the hungry one. He is the naked one. He is the thirsty one. He is the one without a home. He is the one who is suffering. These are our*

treasures, she said, looking at the rows of pallets in the caravanserai. They are Jesus.'
Words of Mother Teresa

Remember, Calcutta is the home of Mother Teresa, an erstwhile nun from the order. I'm being awakened to a world far beyond William and Mary. Yes, convents feature on the hopscotch route, though I'm not all that religious.

School has become my club, my place of leisure with my new Anglo-Indian friends that I've courted regardless of Mother's supposed intellectual frown.

No intellect involved, simply prejudice.

It's winter, time for the cricket season. Father has managed to arrange tickets for the players enclosure at Eden Gardens, the Mecca of cricket in Bengal. All India is mad on cricket so are we,

The cricket field is carpeted with dishy men in their pristine 'whites'. strutting their figure of eight. We have been tasting refreshments galore, spicy puffed rice in newspaper cones now dropped upturned on the ground, and Magnolia ice cream losing its snowy peaks like the Himalayas in climate change. We are now ready for the match. The crowd roars as the team steps out onto the sward with its own colony of live-in pigeons. My new Anglo- Indian friends and I sit with intoxicated attention on the front row, eyes on the players.

As the crowd roars, drums and trumpets accompany with savage, anarchic celebration every ball that reaches the boundary and we jump up from our seats, hoping the players will notice, but they don't.

On the terraces, pulsating their legs with frenzy, their mouth releasing blood-like saliva, the Bengalis masticate the betel, *(paan)* and in the recesses of my garments, I wet my pants. I'm aghast. Tush, girl, why all this quivering of your nether region? For God's sake, it's only a cricket match. I'll clean up when I get home.

Calcutta is a muggy, polluted city; you need regular showers to stay clean. Fortunately, I have talcum powder. I shall strip, and scatter it all over my naked body, now changing shape as in the hands of a sculptor. Bloating nipples, swelling flesh rising from beneath, provides a foretaste not of 'growing up', rather a warning of some advancing disease. Is that what growing up means?

I must not freak out at the thought. I have seen Marilyn Munroe on the screen at my friend's birthday party. I know gentleman prefer boobs and I prefer gentlemen with muscle and a girl needs muscle to climb Everest.

Accepting it will be difficult for players to date a group, I give cricket a miss and go solo and try pole-axing a handsome wrestler, a simian giant with muster and bluster. Staccato heart-beating sequence follows: I pick up a public phone. Surprisingly, he answers the call. Yes, he would meet me at the hotel if I promise him a kiss. I'm both chilled and thrilled. An open door, at last! I hang-up in confusion. I've lost the only opportunity I ever had.

Thank goodness I hung up for I was too simple to recognise that 'lost opportunity' might well be the tentacles of a paedophile. Best to stay virgin.

Then a miracle happens, I find myself in the arms of this tall, handsome man with a dashing moustache who drives a yellow Studebaker. I have slipped into a gang of teen-twenty agers, some wanting a crush, some awaiting marriage, and me still on the hunt.

We strolled on the esplanade of the Hooghly, watching the surviving coach and horses from British India taking tourists for a ride, providing them with just the hint of the Hyde Park of London with men in top hats and ladies in bonnets.

He became my secret boyfriend. It was all so hush hush, and romantic. It lasted all of a summer and a monsoon. I was in love.

Next year will bring in change. Finished with school and hunting down a male, my schedule has changed; I'll be off for teacher training as a teacher in Simla. I chuckle, will a girl like me ever make a responsible teacher?

1955-56

Simla:
British footprints still in India

'Simla 1922. While the rest of India bakes in the hot season, up in the pine-scented coolness of the Himalayan hills, the English have recreated a vision of home. Here are half-timbered houses, amateur theatricals, gymkhanas and a glittering vice-regal court for the socialites. The summer capital of the British Raj is fizzing with the energy of the jazz age.'
Barbara Cleverly: *Ragtime in Simla*.

Eight thousand feet up the Himalayas in Simla, perched on a mountain, you'll find St Bede's Teacher Training College. You may have been told that the sun never sets on the British Empire, but behold, here it has climbed a mountain!

Yes, the ghosts of the British still linger. They climb

the Himalayas, every summer as in days of yore. Yes, it was properly fizzing then but today *Entrez, mes amis* to another Britain. St. Bede's College runs a mighty fleet that still sails the seven seas, with admiral, captains and sailors, all carrying Indian warship identities: INS Dramatic, Olympus and Debate. Though glad to see the HMS preface of the Royal Navy has gone, so I feel extraordinarily privileged to be part of our country's defence, proud to be voted Captain of INS Dramatics

As Captain of Dramatics, I gave myself the opportunity to play Sir Anthony Absolute in Sheridan's, *The Rivals* and took inspiration from Mother. I was able to imitate her haughty mannerisms and her perpetual frown at the lower orders. I stamped my boots to express dominance, though I can't honestly remember how she managed to do the same through those delicate slippers of her sari. So, it came to pass my drama life germinated in St Bede's from a seed sewn long ago by a girl on a skipping rope.

Finally, I put a stamp on my recent independence from Mother; I chopped off my lovely, waist-length hair. It's been a telling epic of promotion, from ringlets, to pigtails, to latest bob. My brown and chestnut locks were Mother's prized possession although each strand was stuck to my head. For the first time the wind filled the sails of liberty and a mountain breeze blew through my hair. It felt like freedom.

As a result, a new, confident, Prami tours the streets of Simla, come the weekend. There's no jazz age now but something else is fizzing. Tour guides swarm with lavish tales of the erstwhile Maharaja and his hundred and something wives all of whom made this giant leap for mankind by filling his palace with children. There's plenty of honey for the guides poking their proboscis into royal scandals. I poke mine and suck honey.

A previous Maharaja manages to elope with the daughter of the British Viceroy from a place now perpetuated as Scandal Point.

'Where's that?' I ask.

'That's exactly where you're standing,' says the man. Too good to be true, to be treading on scandal!

I look around. Far in the distance, its peaks covered in perpetual snow, the mighty Himalayan range stretches along as far as I can turn my neck. I certainly have no wish to be perpetuated in such place, but a pinch of scandal will spice my week end. Then there are secret outings to the cinema with a young Goan lieutenant from the Western Command who were stationed in Simla. We meet at Scandal Point alongside honeymooners strolling hand in hand, but note our cowardice: not daring to be noticed we head for the cinema and when lights go out, we simply hold hands! I'm ashamed of my cowardice. It seemed apposite to be seen feisty and fearless by my crew, a ghost-buster and a damned nuisance to the nuns! A cheerleader of the worst sort. Watch the act of defiance that rings in the new Prami.

I'm challenged to ring the metal hand bell at the top of the stairs, to raise an alarm about a ghost who we believe haunts the corridors. It's a new part to play. I perform it with the gusto of a warden ringing the church bells, warning a village of plague, power cut and pestilence.

'I've seen a ghost in the corridor!'

When the world rushes out, even the nun in charge makes an unseemly appearance, a dressing gown below with a shaved head on top. Pretending to have seen a ghost didn't fool her; she looked like a ghost herself without her habit.

I was packed off for a Court Marshall to Mother Superior; My head could be on the block, but, paying due regard to my status as an officer, she let me off with a warning,

I have need for some comfort eating. I'll gorge myself with cake. But the hand froze even as the mouth opened

'No, No! Don't kill yourself with gluttony'. It's nun-speak for sure that I've picked up. 'You'll ring many more bells in Simla and beyond.

Hold it! Tarry awhile, no question of 'beyond'; it's the here and now that matters. The soil beneath is heating up. Flood waters are rising; clouds of Partition are blackening the sky.

I want to be a participant in the hot spot of history, not hand around with the nuns in Simla. With the British on the run, India on the boil, my parents have ordered me home.

*

I return to Delhi on the choo choo-train on which I had arrived, and say a fond farewell to the mountains that I love. I'm leaving a place of wonder where mighty *deodar* firs reach up to the sky into blackness, into silence.

So tired after the hurly-burley of the past days, silence would be good.

The terrain changes as the train moves on. The air gets scented with freshness; pine cones seem to be sloping off the hillside, with their offering of welcome.

In the distance *Pahari* figures, with baskets slung off their foreheads are on their way home through overgrown monsoon tracks that snake up the mountainside, connecting them to their tiny terraced fields, the terrain too unforgiving and space too limited for growing quality wheat.

They are *Pahari* mountain men, fair-skinned and tall, skin hardened by freezing air, traditional round, woollen hats snugly fitted atop their snowy peaks, and on their lower slopes, even more tightly fitted pyjamas to keep the cold air out. There are some girls following in *salwar kameez*, white tunics above baggy pants with tight pigtails curled round with precision, ending in huge, ribboned bows behind their ears. They must be school girls in uniform going home. I wonder what it means to be a mountain girl. In all my days at the Colonel's library, I never read *Heidi* and her Alpine romance with Peter, the goat herd. My eyes are closing.

The train jerks to a halt. Our midway stop, Solon. I can smell a man frying *pakoras* on the platform, and a group of rosy-cheeked children lining up noisily for drinks, a man in a round woollen hat, traversing the train, with a metal kettle of ready-made sweet, tea that he serves in small earthen pots calling out, '*Chai garam*, hot tea!' He too, is red cheeked; it must be the pure mountain air.

The whistle blows, the guard waves the red flag. Just as the train is ready to leave, an egg-vender rushes in balancing an egg on his nose, not a beggar in this case, but a salesman. Intrigued by the circus act I wave back.

'*Namaste* Humpty Dumpty,' I call out, eyes focussed on the precarious egg. The egg does not fall, the man does not leave, but continues persuading with gurulike certainty on the virtues of the egg. I buy the egg and hold it in my hands, a perfect ova, a work of art to admire. Nevertheless, I gobble up its wisdom and put the little fella to rest.

It gets hotter and hotter as I near the plains. No wonder the British Government made Simla its summer headquarters, shifting its operations *en masse* to the Simla hills, Uncle Tom Cobley and all, their wherewithal being transported eight thousand feet by labouring bullock carts. I look around, no bullocks anywhere; maybe they migrated or simply got eaten like the egg. Such is power, no respecter of bullocks.

Fiddlesticks, Prami, you're not only Nero, but Zero. You pontificate on an egg when the whole of your country is burning.

1947

Delhi: The Partition

'Today, a million daughters cry out to you, Waris Shah,
Rise! O' narrator of the grieving!
Look at your Punjab, Today, fields are lined with
corpses, and blood fills the Chenab.'
Amrita Pritam: *Poems*

Difficult to take in the full horror of Partition.

With millions of Hindus and Muslims on the move, like the Blitz, tragedy strikes home. India becomes free from the British in 1947, one nation divides into two, India and Pakistan and both sides are drenched in the rain of bloodshed that followed.

Lalaji, my paternal grandfather had gone shopping for vegetables in Lahore when a Hindu-manned lorry arrived, collecting urgently all Hindus with homes on

the road as a lorry of Muslims was moving just behind them, clinically murdering each Hindu that they found. They pulled her out, not fully dressed, and carried her off protesting that she would not leave without her husband! Fortunately, they saved Bhabji, my grandmother just in time and searched for her husband in the maze of the city.

Straight after Partition, Delhi becomes a hubble-bubble of criss-crossing communities. On the pavement, food hawkers, hawked; entrepreneurial Punjabi, refugees 'discovered' through sheer 'chance', exotic historical souvenirs, and tried to flog them as treasured possessions of the erstwhile Rajas.

'Snap them up quickly!' they bargained. 'Such a historic opportunity will not last!'

On the road taxis rubber-honked with their incessant belching, like a band in ill repair; scooter rickshaws acquired by young refugees added to the cacophony; they were young Punjabis determined to find work; such a proud race like ours does not beg. Neither did Lalaji. He was busy finding shelter for refugees.

Dispersed family members found their way to Delhi and gathered at the campus of Delhi University. My uncle, Doctor Laroia, a chemistry professor had been allocated this long, rambling bungalow by the university to which different groups of Mother's family entered in dribbles, and the place became a Dickensian menagerie.

First, came grandfather, *Bare Papa*, his wife and three sons, the youngest, six months younger than me. This imperious man with snowy hair and the growl of a huge lion kept on reproducing like a male rabbit! He sired a cricket team from his loins, a cool dozen. On arrival, he set up stage like a Mughal Emperor giving audience, a conqueror, not a refugee. *Salaam Huzur, Salaam Huzur, Salaam, Salaam!* It is obvious that Mother show his genes.

In another wing, Kamala Masi, Mother's favourite widowed sister made her home with her children, albeit with the regular posse of Mother, Hari ayah and me who arrive daily on a clickety, horse-drawn *tonga* from The Grand Hotel, where we lodge, not so grandly. Anticipating Hindi emerging as the *lingua franca* in the new India. Mother has enrolled me in Queen Mary's Hindi medium school to learn to speak better Hindi than her! I don't know about better Hindi, but my English has certainly gone *phut*. From a gifted pupil, hungry to read, I now have *Babar the Elephant* placed in front of me. Understanding my frustration Kamla Masi brings me suitable novels from the America United States Information Service library where she works, and my education continues regardless of the curious fact that a girl, so brilliant in English, is taught everything in Hindi! Barring that anomaly, the rest of school life was fun.

Here kites sweep down from our neem trees and steal our chapatis as we take our break on the benches in the playground, all hilarious fun. Although I cannot say the same about the rest my curriculum but have nothing but praise for the lady in charge of my new home.

Kamla Masi's was the nourishment I needed in the early years of my growing up. She's more of a mother to me than my own and these two years with her brought about a momentous change in my life. At last, I was in the heart of the rough and tumble of family life, with children's tittle-tattle and laughter. I became Prami of free abandon at a time India was burning.

I cannot finish this account without celebrating the scratched dining table in Kamla Masi's home; some of it was useful for home work, ludo, snakes and ladders, but it also was a sanctum for Kamla Masi. Daily, she sits at one end reading our holy book, the *Bhagwat Gita*. I look over her shoulder, and she explains my religion in simple ways that I can understand, and slowly I gain knowledge of my culture, the history, mythology, the struggle and its faith. It is Kamla Masi who made me truly Indian and all that I saw I saw during Partition made me grow up.

We were all together in the house when the news of the assassination of Mahatma Gandhi reached us. It spread like wildfire across the houses. Families emerged from their pods and we all gathered together in a room, most people sobbing and crying, a shared ocean of grief. I was submerged within it, and drowned in the flooding tide. I felt its power but couldn't really understand it. I was only a child.

But today, I have to ask myself, Did India become better after such a huge sacrifice? The mirror cracked from side to side, but would a better India emerge? It's a moot point to ponder, how much did India gain after Independence? Does British influence still survive? The answer must be, yes, yes, sadly, yes. It survives in the likes of me.

> *'People brought up just like me have ruled India since 1947, perpetuating a twisted continuance of colonial rule. I would go as far as to say that my generation of Indians was possibly more colonized than those who lived in colonial times and our tragedy was that most of us lived out our lives without ever finding out.'*
> Tavleen Singh: *Durbar*

It was difficult for a youngster to conceive the brutality of the horror on such a scale but it all strikes home when I tell you of the experience of a single person, Kamla Masi's daughter, Prabha.

At the time of Partition, she was a boarder at the Sacred Heart Convent in Lahore, now in Pakistan. Threats were around that if any Hindu student was discovered within its walls, the college would be razed to the ground and every nun within massacred in retribution.

Prabha was their only Hindu student and the nuns feared that her presence might well be public knowledge. She needed to be spirited out in haste, but how to get her beyond the walls, who to trust.

In the end they put their faith in an Anglo-Indian contact who, being Christian, was possibly safe from execution. The good man accepted this dangerous rescue. Somehow, he got Prabha over the wall; he got her a third-class ticket and put the terrified girl, only seventeen, to take her chances into an over-packed train. He telegrammed her mother to await her arrival in Delhi, fearing, only too realistically, that she might find her dead.

All trains were being combed thoroughly by slit-throat maniacs. It was her Kismet she escaped detection by crouching low behind her small bag. Train after train pulled in with the dead and dying amidst a background of groaning, coughing and blood-spluttering. To this day Prabha does not know who this good angel was; he vanished like a ghost into the night and even the nuns never saw him again.

More than half a century later, Prabha discovers the train ticket and we post it back to the nuns as a memento of her eternal gratitude. Today, Prabha is my emotional umbrella with WhatsApp connecting us however far apart we may be, for we're bonded as if living next door.

1957

Cambridge at last

After a long stint at Queen Mary' School I was brought back to Calcutta to start my degree in English at Loreto College. That's the easy part. During those years I also applied to Cambridge for which I had to take a demanding entrance exam that involved detailed knowledge of the Bible and the Greats in classical literature, all way beyond the remit of the Calcutta University curriculum.

Mother kiboshed the idea of Cambridge, to be expected, but Father agreed that he would help me if took the responsibility of doing all the preparation without any help. Perhaps, he wanted to make a man of me! For the first time he went counter to Mother. I busted my balls to get there. Then time came for the results. I waited in hope, crossed my fingers and toes and if my breasts could do it, I would push their button! Just one little letter from Girton to make me a swan. Fate was on my side; St Jude was my guide; he's a patron of hopeless cases. This time he listened. Who dares, must win. To my astonishment, an offer arrived. My life in Cambridge is about to begin.

I stare at Mother in triumph. Reluctantly, she has admitted defeat, but there's still no sight of a white flag, not even that sometime smile.

'Make sure, you behave.'

*

We set off to Cambridge in October of 1957 through countryside of golden haystacks piled in fields, a season of mists over yellowness. We were driven there by an avuncular taxi driver in a brownish tweed jacket, and yellowish teeth matching the autumn country side. He was truly my garrulous host. I had mentioned my excitement at going to Cambridge and ooed and aahed about the countryside around, made alive by Rupert Brooke who took me to this place of magic where hares come out about the corn ere night is born. He had never heard of Rupert Brooke. Our driver lacks a soul.

'Next March you'll see the March hares boxing. It's the mating season.'

'Ahoy!'

I'm quick on cue. His eyes twinkle. He may not have a soul, but he reads mine.

'You'll get your chance in Cambridge. The ratio of boys to girls is 7:1.'

I stifle a chuckle; Mother deepens her frown. Unfortunately, I'd never learnt to box, a right hook at Mother would have left her panting in the ring. It's time for tea, so we rev up the taxi and drive straight into Rupert

Brook relaxing in the village of Grantchester, exactly the way I had imagined.

> *'Stands the Church clock at ten to three?*
> *And is there honey still for tea?'*
> Rupert Brooke: *The Old Vicarage, Granchester*

Yes, there's honey still for tea. Yes, the tea tastes delicious and scones melt like manna, if manna tastes like scones. The autumn sun is low, and the branches are changing colour to orange gold, a black bird sings its vespers and back in the mountains, St Bede's parades its marching song.

> *'Come, cheer up, my lads, 'tis to glory we steer,*
> *To add something more to this wonderful year.'*
> David Garrick: *Heart of Oak*

*

I can remember the first sight of my college, the mock Gothic facade of Girton at the end of the driveway. I have looked at so many pictures on the prospectus but this is more impressive, like a stately home with wrap-around lawns and a meadow of sheep to the right with a formal courtyard in the middle to park cars. Inside, I have read, is a room full of embroidery. Girly stuff, not of interest but maybe, somewhere, up there, in some college, a man will be waitin…

It wasn't a man; it was a woman.

She's a short business-like lady, with very short, greyish hair. I learn later she is known as the 'general', very appropriate and military for her 'command and control' nature. After the briefest of greeting, she indicates to my parents to sit down. I remain standing. Her office is a no-nonsense place too. Information on the wall is hung and quartered.

I hope I've not swopped my Mother for another act-alike alike Mother Superior. I'm told she lives nearby in Girton Village, a well-known, sturdy figure, ever on a bicycle, pumping her legs with intent.

During our meeting she drops a bomb. I have missed seven days of term, courtesy of Asian flu, and I shall not be allowed to go home until all those days are made up. I'm smirk-faced; it doesn't matter a toss. I have got into my college, and there I would like to sleep the night... with someone delicious, peut-être?

'It's not just a matter of passing exams,' the general explains the rules, 'in order to qualify for a degree you have to sleep the required number of nights within Cambridge.'

Goodbye Mother. Now, aren't I glad Father will take you back to London, and I'm saved your triumphant valediction,

'Prami, you deserve any punishment you get.'

Three ebony elephants will trumpet on the windowsill of my study. The stage is set; may the plot thicken.

1957-1958

Salad days

'My Salad days when I was green in judgement.'
Shakespeare: *Antony and Cleopatra*

Meet the new Prami, a slim, first year, sari-clad student, ripened to a glow in the Indian sun. There's an élan vital, a Perky-Quirky quality about her. Not many girls sweep along King's Parade in Cambridge on a green Raleigh bike, sari blowing in the wind. Off the bike her rounded hip beneath her sari suggests curves that would make any belly dancer proud. Cut a dash, young woman, go for adventure and daring. Allow your navel to keep peeping. Life is expectation, exhilaration and riotous energy. Whichever way you look. The oxygen in the English Department burns brightest in the fifties. One moment you're in a convent, the very next the world beckons. It's the hopscotch masterplan.

The English Department is a fountain that overflows. I shall walk through Paradise with Milton and never lose it, even take Marvell to bed, invoking carnal bliss.

> *'Let us roll all our strength and all*
> *Our sweetness up into one ball,*
> *And tear our pleasures with rough strife*
> *Thorough the iron gates of life.'*
> Andrew Marvell: *To his Coy Mistress*

Maybe, answer the call of sophistication at the wine tasting society. So clearly, I remember the wobbling girl cycling home, belly bouncing with Chablis or was it Chateauneuf du Papey? No question of tasting, I swallowed gulps of the gleeful stuff. Life is both expectation and exhilaration, except for lack of friends.

Even though familiar with British children from the tennis courts of childhood, I found myself within an alien tribe in Girton that keeps its distance. I had hoped to have plunged into a student melee on arrival, but British students don't engage with me at all; the girls have already formed cosy groups with their coterie of private school boyfriends. Perhaps I arrived here too late, curse the Asian flu. Looking around the twittering groups. I'm not likely to fit in with these kinds of people. What's within me is dynamic, but put me in a group, I'm poor little Prami.

I hear a shout from within. What happened to the girl who rang the bell?

To my rescue came St Bede's and its naval ethos. Captains of ships do not bend; they rise to their strength. In my case it's ping-pong, just as prestigious as Wimbledon and certainly given due regard all over South-East Asia. Now Girton does not have a table tennis team, yet most of the men's colleges do; they even hold regular events, a bit social, a little competitive. It will open many doors.

Now here's a chance to spread my wings, the venue rotating weekly between colleges. The world's my oyster. I shall pry it open with my ping-pong bat.

The horizon opens, enthusiasm flares. I advertise on the notice board and to my surprise pull out a Hungarian from my own college to make a twosome Girton squad, ready to paint the town red.

Meet Eva from Hungary. When the advancing Russian army flooded Budapest, student revolutionaries were forced to escape, leaving their families behind. Eva would never return to Hungary again and was a refugee for life. She too has found cold comfort at Girton but is not isolated like me. Along with her other Hungarian students several scientific, some mathematical, who were hosted by Cambridge one to each college. They were the crème de la crème of their country, and one, Robbie from Christ's is more than happy to shake my hand.

As well as interest in ping-pong, there was commonality between Eva and me. England was never to her taste; she hated their pathetic dishes that trespassed as 'food' and longed for her Hungarian goulash, remembering what a range of paprika was available to her mother. I measured up by boasting of curries that would pander to her taste, albeit I know nothing about cooking; just pile the on the stuff, blast and burst. Fortunately, Eva didn't die.

My friendship with Eva was rather special; she too looked at England from an outsider's point of view in a way an Anglophile like me had never noticed. She found their small talk superficial, unnecessary twittering, that made them boring, conventional and uninteresting. What about Indians, I enquired? There was no curiosity whatsoever; I suppose in a communist nation the outside world is locked away. Nevertheless, she had chosen modern languages to read as she enjoyed the buoyancy of Italian speech, although she herself was rather dour. Eva was plain with buck teeth and forthright manner, unlike the sweater girls of the fifties, like the popular Doris Day. Eva replaced pointy breasts with a simple T-shirt.

Next to Eva lived the flamboyant Janet Ashworth, a total contrast. She seems a hippy before the era of hippies. With her long, blonde hair falling carelessly on her shoulders, she looks so casual and careless when compared to the coiffured styles of modern students.She sits on her bed, legs curled up in lotus position, and may well drawl out Baudelaire in her breathy voice.

> *'With wine, with poetry, or with virtue, as you chose.*
> *But get drunk.'*
> Charles Baudelaire, *Paris Spleen*

His words bond with the moodiness of dimmed lights further enhanced by coloured cloth around the lamp. I have never seen one like her. Janet is an exhibitioner in modern languages and will slip into French without warning as she sips the Swiss potage while Eva attempts her throaty Italian. This is totally a new world for me.

Shall I babel-up the soup with a few masala croutons?

Janet joins our soup group and we celebrate midnight with a toast to Knorr's great achievement.

Today is Janet Ashworth's day to host the poulet beverage on the top floor with its sloping roof and a dormer window. A song reaches me even before I enter; its Edith Piaf's voice singing '*Je ne regrette riens.*' When I step in, it's like entering an arty-farty attic world; little sketches on paper and posters line the walls. Her favourite seems to be Chagall and his creations, imitated or exaggerated. At one side they are humorous cartoonish sketches of animals, mainly cats, and dingle-dangle multi-coloured beads hang on hooks.

We are starting a soup group for regular evening meetings in each other's rooms.

Next, it will be my turn. As for my room, I take no credit for special effects Ethnicity is provided by the colourful, Rajasthani paisley bedcover with embroidered Kashmiri bolsters rolling on the bed like plump oriental sausages. Now everyone could recline maharaja style and pay heed when I take over.

My contribution is often to illuminate my country. I'm distressed by their lack of knowledge. How to be diplomatic, yet inform them they are ignorant?

I choose the right stories with an indulgent smirk. Our great Krishna Menon, freedom fighter and learned statesman was once invited to make a speech to The United Nations. At dinner, a politician who shall not be named, is sitting beside him. With affected show of camaraderie, the man turns to him when the first course is removed, 'Likee soupeee?'

When Menon finishes his epic eight-hour speech on Kashmir, he turns politely to his neighbour, 'Likee speechee?' he enquires.

'Would you believe,' I say with diplomacy 'People still think we're living on trees!'

We exchange views, massage politics with wit, and 'gen-up' on latest publications, quite like the Bloomsbury group. The quirky mixture of our international trio adds spice to the simple Knorr soup.

Memories, memories. memories! Sometimes, sad memories.

'Eva, this slice of birthday cake is for you, for I know well you have a sweet tooth. When I visited you in Italy for the last time, you sent me home with a box of Baci Perugina, Perugian kisses. Passengers on the train took the 'mic', blowing me kisses from across the aisle. I can do the same; send a kiss to whichever space you inhabit. You're an atheist, so I bring flowers to your grave.'

'Dearest Janet, I cannot offer you cake for tears drench the slice in my hand. You passed away with multiple sclerosis Yet, memories are also made of sorrow and must be cherished. You will ever remain with me, a lurking smile.'

The first term rolls on, now pleasantly punctuated by lectures by day, then cycling back to Girton after pinging and ponging, and Janet returning from thronging gigs; I'm not alone anymore.

1957 winter

Cambridge: Mad dogs and Indian girls go out in the freezing frost

Come Christmas, I'm alone, even the dons have taken off. My bedroom is freezing; they turn down the heat at night. Post-war frugality. The fog outside tries to squeeze me in further. I've never experienced four o'clock darkness. I look out of the windows, see nothing, but I know Girton sheep are munching in Girton pastures. Well, it's their kind of weather. There's a spooky darkness about the place. I hear a crackling, on the window pane, perhaps the elephants warning me, 'Prami you've made a mistake.' I look towards the window. The sandalwood pair are silent, yet their heady perfume warms my nostrils, taking me back home.

As my hand stretches for a cholate biscuit, I knock over a Christmas card from Janet. It's a painting by Chagall.

There are two lovers afloat among bright blue clouds in a ballet-like *pas de deux*. Below, a faint suggestion of people of the world, all represented in dream-like soft shades. She has even added a little sketch of a turkey with a chef's hat, with the tag line, *Salut la dinde Mulligatawny*. She has gone home to her family in the vicarage, yet she still throws out a laugh at me. Taking comfort from this *voix de deux*, I grab a chicken sandwich. I shall join her in a Christmas feast and make it a party. Better still, why not go to a party. There must be plenty in town.

I leave the elephants to their own devises and set off. Girton is a maze of corridors with just the odd light sprinkled about, the whole place seems like a morgue with bodies in each of the frozen rooms. I must pull my coat tight lest one escape.

My imagination has gone into overdrive. Never have I ever been alone at night. Take a chance, young woman, take a chance woman, take a chance; you might even get invited.

I venture out into the night. Thank you, Mother for all the woollies I resisted; it's freezing. When I return, I'll tuck into my dark green, Rajasthani velvet quilt and curl up like a foetus.

Market Square looms dark and soulless except for a black cat that appears mysteriously hidden in the dark. I can hear laughter and music somewhere behind the shops. It must be a pub or something.

I can't see clearly through the frosted glass, so open the glass door a tiny little bit, and peek into that florescent room… Don't like this place, full of awful tubular steel furniture. But there are young people all around; the boys are snazzy and jazzy with tight, skinny trousers, suede shoes with white socks deliberately displayed; jackets, with large square collars bordered with velvet, the necessary buttoned waistcoat. On top there is the regulation Tony Curtis hairdo, though a few have long, sleek sides. I follow my eyes down to their suede brothel creepers. For going where, I wonder. Here's one smoking with 'attitude' and listening to Elvis pumping out *Jailhouse Rock*. But where are the girls?

They are right by the music, rock'n'roll with their partners in ballooning yards of skirt. Would I could join them. Wouldn't I just?

In Calcutta when rock'n'roll arrived, Anglo-Indian youngsters jived down cinema aisles. Verboten for the likes me. All I could do was to watch from a folding seat. Now, here's my chance. I step one foot in and halt abruptly. What if one of them sees me! These are Teddy boys. I've been already warned about them in India. I step back quietly, shutting the door.

This smart *arse* is a farce, with the bravado of a craven desperado; inside I'm jelly. I've already been warned.

'Be careful; there are town and gown fights in Cambridge.'

What will happen if I get caught by the powers that be? As in Western movies so popular in India now the law can suddenly turn up, blowing whistle, seizing, dragging, arresting… I'd better get out!

Adventures are not meant to end with a blimp. I return to Girton and check in with the night porter. We're allowed exeat till midnight; It's only nine o'clock.

Excitedly, I tell him what I've seen, but, he's no mincer of words.

'Stupid, Miss Lal, you could have ended up in jail!'

I'm taken aback.

'I shall go with a proper group next time.' His voice is stern.

'Let there never be a next time, Miss Lal.'

I leave, being put into my place, good and proper by a porter. I look over my shoulder, mouthing a silent retort,

'There's sure to be a next time, Sir.'

1957

Cambridge: Poppy Day

Olé! The eleventh hour of the eleventh day of the eleventh month. when the guns fell silent and the Great War was won.

Time to ring another bell. This year, I've taken charge of the Girton float and allowed my crazy mind the go-ahead. Like a circus approaching, I shall bring Moulin Rouge to town with rattling of cash-loaded buckets as band-*baja*.

I'm told the whole University goes wild on this rag day. Thousands gather as King's Parade carnivals with outrageous abandon with colourful bunting criss-crossing the road; girls in hula hoops rotating; guitarists strumming popular songs like '*The Good Ship, Venus.*' To be expected. Of course, for it rhymes with penis. On the same subject, a man in black tails, top hat but no trousers might take a bow and ask you a favour! Don't shock. Just be prepared for Poppy Day abandon.

It's a costume extravaganza; cross-dressing is a must, the dafter the costume, the whakier the action. Victorian murderers come to life, see matadors with pantomime bulls in strife; a hunky nurse pushes a funky student in a pram with a bottle in his mouth, and of course, the zaniest of all, the Girton float full of wannabe courtesans, shrilling for a kiss with an après St. Bede director, aching to be noticed. I'm dressed in tight trousers with a piercing V neck, revealing just a bit, suggesting much more.

We call out from the float, 'A shilling for a kiss!' We call out. 'Make it two-bob for a classy one."

Students leap up to get lip-smacked, lipstick-whacked for a fully paid kiss!

After all, love is never cheap. As the float moves on with our girls shrieking to Offenbach music. I call out again, 'Make the most of your kisses while you can.' It applies to mee as well. Now is the time to capture my man.

A little hitch along the way. High-kicking girls with frilly pantaloons were easy to find. What turned out more difficult to acquire was Toulouse Lautrec.

Once my bearded Hungarian wonder realises no kisses would be coming as he's not amused. 'I'd rather be 'too loose' than Toulouse.'

Not so me; Robbie from Hungry, I'm still a one-man woman, sans man.

One thinks of the sixties as a tearaway era, but the fifties beat to a better drum. Shucks to the wartime economy; young people have the right to start dancing. It's all a question of entitlement, earned from the Union Jack.

The war is over; young people need a proper release; I need a gung-ho response from the young. And I got it, and I got a man, as well. A group of students went rampant beneath me. From the lorry I signalled them to earn a few shillings. With ribaldry, they hoisted a man on their shoulders and almost threw him into my arms.

And, thus ends the *Captain of Dramatic's* log book on successful seduction.

1958

Lent term

The Lent term starts with a bang. 'Do you want to go to a bottle party?' asks Eva in her matter-of-fact way.

'It might be not your kind of place, but my Hungarian friend, Robbie who's based in Christ's, informs me there is a man from his college who has taken a fancy to you; he's an exhibitioner and like you, is reading English. He's seen you in action on Poppy Day and describes you as woman of abandon.' Not a flattering commendation. I'm just a freedom-bound woman with a dash of sass, but after a lack-lustre Christmas, I'm game for anything.

'Who is he?' I can barely hide my excitement.

'Don't hang about,' he warns me. 'Bill Le Hunte has already got three girlfriends in tow. One at home in Bristol, a cousin in Wales and the third, a German student right under your nose.'

A right old Lothario, eh? Piracy is required to grapple his boat; I'm not the sort of who takes prisoners. By the end of term, they'll be out!

New term, new beginning!

A kind of thrill buzzes within. I have the bit between the teeth as we set off for Christ's College, cycling into the chasing rain.

The exodus of Girtonians in their green and white striped scarves is a nightly sight on Huntington Road. We're all in gowns for it's mandatory to wear them after dark. Just imagine, large black bat wings flapping in the air as they catch the wind blowing in from the fens.

Off we go past large houses with slivers of light slicing the ground-floor curtains and darkened gardens that in daytime show a riot of autumn footprints.

The odd cypress tree stands sentinel, its dark silhouette just catches the light from the porch. Someone has planted a row of sweet peas; a whiff is carried to me as I slowly wield my bicycle... till we reach Castle Hill and pause.

Ahead in the river to our left, the punts are safely moored by the bridge, a streetlamp reflects in the water, quivering slightly, and on the right, St. John's College looms ahead, now dark and forbidding; some choristers are heading for the chapel.

All is peaceful and silent apart from the water lapping gently on the side of the punts, and a creak or two from the moorings. Nevertheless, this is danger country! Proctor and bulldogs prowl the streets every night; it behoves you to always carry your gown when you leave Girton in the morning. The proctor might approach, doff his hat, 'Madam, are you a member of the University?'

You have two alternatives: if you are guilty, either pay a fine, or run. Most men run, chased by bulldogs who are speedy runners trained by the police. The wise man dives into a college, the slow one gets caught. Now, how can I run in a sari? The dither-factor ramps up as we near the college, I tell myself to take control, be a captain of the ship once again. Time to ring that bell.

The noise from the party floods out from the first-floor window like a burst dam. Who are the dam busters within? Many of them will be returnees from National Service; they must be freedom fighters; worthy of the Union Jack they served for two years. Worthy of me?

A bottle party for a bottled-up woman

I pound. We've reached the party. I'm ready for the 'real gird my loins, tighten my sari. In for a rupee, in for a thing', if only I knew what 'real thing' means.

The room seems very plain from the little I can see through choking, engulfing smoke. the light is kept deliberately low as Bill Hailey and his Comets thump really loud. The tang of 'wine-allsorts', fills the air. So many bottles lie vanquished on the floor.

Behold live drama on a stage already set when the curtain goes up: entwined, snogging couples, one with red wine balanced in his hand pours it into the mouth of a girl with lips of a matching colour as his fingertips scan her thighs.

In the middle of the room a blondie tart poses on a man's lap both, taking turns to finish off the fizzy white wine. Her cleavage is the main recipient.

Along the wall a shaky, scorch-marked table seems drunk as well where people have set down cigarettes, and split splodges of wine to 'groom' it for the night that must inevitably follow. One thing is certain; nothing here is romantic. I could even agree with Mother; it's obscene.

There's no place to move, shall I call a retreat and lower the flag? Like I did with the Teddy boys? Just then Robbie materialises from the fog and like a ghost from Styx ferries me to a living male.

'Here's the man you have come to meet.'

How disappointing! From the back I can see a worn-out tweed jacket with leather patches at the elbows, slender, long fingers pressing a dent into a 'roll your own' fag; a laid-back human, totally in contrast to the manly body I wanted. I notice a slight nick on his chin. Perhaps the razor slipped, or the hand trembled or he got up too late from his bed. I have been told by Robbie of his eyrie, a dim room with pulled curtains, from where his somnambulant lens decodes from above the hustle of the main street below. It's important to know, who is town, who is gown? Perhaps, a foreign language student to pounce on? I've been told he already has three girlfriends in tow.

Not impressive, at first glance but I've been told that he's been demobbed from the RAF, not as a pilot, but a trainee spy! Now that makes him intriguing. The Cold War is on, remember; I may have got myself another James Bond!

Reckless abandon, come hither. Your education has begun; It's the same fellow who fell on my lap on Poppy Day! Life is full of surprises, let's see what awaits. 'Knock-knock, who's there?' He's not there. He continues to stare at his empty bottle. How can Eva have got it so wrong?

He's clearly not for grabs. How can I get this moribund to flirt? Beautiful red sari, a come-hither pansy staring provocatively behind my ear will not do the job. I'll now have to put my put my stumbling social skills to work? His half-open eyes didn't even blink at Robbie's introduction. Yet, there's that half smile still lurking on his face; Poppy Day memory, perhaps? I'll take it as cue.

*

'Hi, pleased to meet you, Bill. Do you enjoy Cambridge?'

'It's a place.' At least, I got the single liner, albeit an abrupt conversation-stopper. Pointing to the revellers behind us, I widen my smile.

'You seem to have so many friends.'

'Some are, some are not.' I sincerely hope these are not. Can't see myself splashing drink on my sari or twining my legs round anyone's trousers. Such company is not for me but I can't walk away so early before the battle has begun. I'm not impressed by the mand but there is a possibility else Robbie would not have acted as a go-between.

However, he has chosen English as his subject, so a possible meeting of minds. I try a different route, hoping we'd connect.

'I've never seen you at lectures.'

'Probably not. I only go the ones I need.'

How the hell do I ever get him to talk; perhaps when he is sober? I invite him to the Girton ball. 'It will be better than cakes and ale', I suggest, 'and bring a flower for my bosom when you arrive.'

I know he'll come. We both know our Shakespeare.

No easy ride to get so far, no hand to hold, no compass to steer, just the skills of the Artful Dodger, pickpocketing life wherever it is scattered. I can't wait for the bull to charge. Olé!

1958

The Girton Ball

Bill arrives on time, washed down and shampooed he looks a different man. He ambles the border, fag in hand and carries nothing to declare bar a rose. Slim, long and lanky, his dinner jacket is to the manor born, but I well know it's rented. I have put his rose in my hair to look 'princessy' and provocative, and quite by chance it matches my pink sari. The stage is set. Between wine and nibbles, I can start my practised routine, I shall edge up to him and dust off any debris from his knee.

'My father too studied in Bristol' (Truth) 'And so did his father.' (True again.)

I tell him I've been to Bristol to visit my uncle where he too was an undergraduate studying engineering.

'Beautiful place,' I say. 'Bristol truly has strong family connections. I race along breathless, and from nowhere drop a bombshell, unplanned, unexpected. Like a script gone haywire.

'I'd like to get married there.'

(Pregnant pause.) He raises an eyebrow quizzically and responds for the first time.

'In the Avon Gorge, I presume?'

'Gorgeous scene' I reply. He's seen through me; I've made a fool of myself.

I open another bottle, get 'spoony' just and as in an Indian movie, yawn and pretend to be just a little bit tipsy and lower my head gently on his lap. I wait for Bill to stroke my hair when suddenly he rises. The single candle by the window starts to flutter; Bill gets up and blows it out.

'It's better dark,' he mutters quietly in his rich voice.

'What is better dark?' I get excited. Is he going to make the first move?

'You don't want your curtains burnt,' he explains prosaically.

I'm not just disappointed, but hugely put off. My plan has blown off with the light. But, did I really want more on our first night?

As he's already standing up, I join him. Together, we take the dishes to the 'gyp' room, that's the shared kitchen for our corridor. Hazel, from my corridor is in there with her boyfriend. I introduce Bill with a testy smile.

'This is Bill from Bristol and Christ's. I reckon, he's the guest for tonight.'

I've put it bluntly and rudely; my irritation shows in my face. Haze reads between the lines, and she steps in like a trooper.

'You can have another guest tomorrow night, if you wish, Prami. Bill won't mind. I'm sure he has plenty of camp followers of his own. Don't you, my handsome soldier?' She sidles up and pecks on his cheek.

'Yes, I have three, but Prami must already know that from Eva.' He stares me in the face knowingly. 'You women always gossip, don't you?'

'All ladies in waiting, eh?' Hazel teases.

'No!' He sounds firm. Supper's over. Only sweets are waiting.

He puts his arm around me and guides me back. In the corridor we hear the band playing a languid tune. The couples must be dancing cheek to cheek. Now must come the awaited moment. I tremble in anticipation.

Bill doesn't waste any time. I stiffen as Bill makes his move, but it's difficult to disentangle a six-yard sari, it turns back on itself into a cocoon; every move is problematic; it's wiggle-proof, struggle resistant. It's a warning I'm crossing my line.

I tell Bill gently; we've got to know each other first. Around the crumpled silk sari, I enquire yet again of friends in Bristol and with consummate skill, he turns the query around to Wales, fetching me stories of the annual haymaking in rural Pembrokeshire, just hinting at high-jinks in haystacks with boys and girls awash with fresh home-brewed beer. I get jealous; perhaps, that's exactly what he intends. All the while he's making his own hay; his hands are busy, and I've not even been aware. My body yearns, the moment is taking over with an onrush of desire, exhilaration and expectation… and fear. Before things get out of hand, I whisper,

'Not tonight, my love… another time.'

'When then Prami?' he demands. 'You've taken no time to get me here. No bloody cake, no effing ale!'

His tongue lashes out with irritation, his body is quivering muscle, and uptight genes. He stays just long enough to cover himself and leaves without a word.

Gone is the evening of wine and roses, gone my very first Adonis. What I get to see is the unbridled power of an unfulfilled man. Do I really want him? I wind my discarded sari around me like a toga and lower myself down to the nuptial couch. Next time, I'll get to know him better.

*

Bill deflowered me the next night in total silence. He entered my room, silhouetted against the light in the corridor. Hazel eyeballs locked onto brown, the unblinking gaze of the demon lover.

'Tonight,' he announced with authority.

The bugle sounded, and with what power came the onslaught: a sudden blow, no preamble, no delay, only consummate conquest. I ended up a hypnotised spectator of my own enslavement.

Never did I suspect that within me lurked those delicious reservoirs of passion, but can I fall in love with this one? Only time will tell.

We both enjoy Cambridge countryside, and during one of our strolls in search of the fen's beautiful sunsets, we found ourselves in a Monet canvas still vibrant with the call of summer. Here we talked, here we loved, here we got to know one another. What different beginnings we had. Bill's father died early. As a result, he was always late for school, for it became his responsibility to light the fire in the living room. And there was I with Hari ayah even pulling up my socks.

But does independence make one any the wiser, or does carrying on being a baby stop one from thinking for oneself? For me it was the here and now that mattered.

I had no vision for tomorrow and being an only child did not help the prima donna ego, and today it's the same thing; the poppy field gives meaning to life.

> *Eternity is passion, girl or boy*
> *Cry at the onset of their sexual joy*
> *'For ever and for ever'; then awake*
> *Ignorant what Dramatis personae spake.*
> W.B. Yeats: *Supernatural songs*

What really got me closer was Bill's love of Wales, the Pembrokeshire that Aunty Herbert and he shared. He would describe the great Atlantic so covered in fog that it made ancient Celtic people believe that beyond the horizon lay the end of the world.

Like Desdemona, I loved him for his stories. Pembrokeshire folk can sleep snug in in their bed thanks to the mighty ocean for protection. They could enjoy their Christmas with home-brewed beer, jugged hare, and cottage-shaking singing.

Although his grassy hills exposed by the retreating glaciers were nothing like the jungles of my Mosaboni, they woke to the same call; the lark rising in the fields and junglee fowl darting about in bushes come sunrise.

And love rising to a climax as the breezes from the fens caressed.

'Darling Billjoo, when we make love, let it always be open to the skies.'

I'm falling in love, for sure.

Think, little Prami. **Think**! This little piggy is building her house on sand.

Not to be thwarted by warning, I still carry on. Bill is inquisitive by nature and wants to know all about my life in India; my family, my lifestyle, my lust for learning and how it all started at the library of the Victoria club.

'Doesn't sound like any football club I know, 'said Bill, it's rugby the Welsh enjoy.'

'No not that sort of club, silly. Clubs are elite institutions. Only the high-end of society is allowed in. What was your father?

'A bank clerk'.

I am silent So the summer term carries on with a lot of how's your father', as Bill puts it. I'm putty in his hands.

*

Today, I've received a devasting airmail from Father informing me that they are now receiving marriage proposals from notable families and have already started a shortlist of suitable boys. Rather, they're putting me on notice. Predicting problems arising at my end, Father has put in a caveat that marriage will only happen after my degree.

So far, I've always tossed aside this insane wish any time marriage-talk was approached. I've have not climbed a summit just to turn around to doggie-follow them back, tail between my legs.

It's almost monsoon time in India, dark clouds gathering to signal the end of hot weather, but for me the heat is just beginning. The long summer vacation arrives in a few weeks, and the sword of Damocles is hovering. I shall be dragged back home. Madness seizes me. I want to put parents on notice. I've already made my choice dear Father; I've chosen the best man in Cambridge. I told Bill the same.

'That's crazy, Prami,' Bill is quick to respond, 'We hardly know each other.'

'Now, which parent won't wait?' I explain. 'Had you had only been from a better home; my parents would have embraced you and treated you like a god and you could have spent the rest of your life on clover.'

'But I'm already lying on clover my dear.' He clears away some fallen poppies, 'Come, lay yourself beside me, Your Majesty.' He twirls the red gown of a poppy, glorious as Elizabeth with her circular white ruff and starts tickling my navel with a blade of long grass.

'You're not taking me seriously, my darling.'

'Trust uncle Bill, I'll find an answer.'

Without a second thought I put my trust in uncle Bill. I need no persuasion when Bill sneaks me out from Girton to Walton-on-the-Naze on the Essex coast where Arjun is conceived by the seaside. Plastic buckets and spades populate the flat, sandy beach where children build their castles by the pier and the North Sea blows the seagulls through the air. I become a marmorised loony, ready to be sculpted. We make long and lasting love by the headland as the incoming tide froths and freezes our toes.

1958

The Bad and the Beautiful

I remember the exact moment when a gynaecologist broke the news. I had gone with Janet on our favourite jaunt along the ladies' mile in Oxford Street. Janet loved to rummage among second-hand books however dog-eared or stained. She might pick up an errant page that had slipped away from its binding and gave voice to its words in her languid way. She could spend hours within book shops and often I joined her, but this time I needed to slip away arranging to meet later for I had made an appointment to consult a doctor at a nearby private clinic for I had noticed the onset of some strange sort moodiness that is totally unlike me.

I headed for the clinic. All around one could hear a Babel of tongues that spelt tourist, and the warm lamb kebabs on sale smelt the same. I've always loved the stuff, yet my stomach turned. I had a dark suspicion of what was to come.

Within the surgery all was hushed expectancy. An

expensively coiffured lady, belly-high with child, was patting briskly the bump inside. Or was she slapping it for daring to be born.

'Poor baby, I thought,' feeling broody. 'What a future for this unborn infant?'

Just then the door opened and a very pleasant doctor examined me. At the end of a routine investigation, she holds out her hand.

'Congratulations, Madam, happy to tell you, you are pregnant.'

She smiled as I remained silent, the lighting had struck like a bolt, even though I knew it was coming. It was clear that the doctor read it on my face.

'I think, you'd better talk to your family,' she said kindly, putting arm round my shoulder.

What family?

My poor parents; how would they dare show their face to anyone? I have landed my whole family in disgrace. I got to know later that Father's brother came wept on his shoulder, tears shared, but nothing spared of my ignominy. Debased and exposed, I'm a pariah in my own country. The tacky beach had done its job.

Mindlessly, I wandered the street, stepping into some baby shop where I bought a bundle of clothes and hugged it close to my chest as one would an infant.

'You didn't deserve to be born to a woman like me, a child of devastation.'

Now I have to face Bill. Will he walk out leaving me to hold the bundle, quite literally?

It turns out it doesn't seem to matter at all. Bill fiddles through my shopping.

'No nappies?' he observes and, on further reflection, he adds. 'I suppose you don't require them in India I expected a different reaction, maybe shock, maybe horror. Not bloody *sangfroid*. No mention of the baby, just the shopping. I'm outraged, my hormones take over.

'You bloody fool!' I shout. 'You know perfectly well I don't plan to go back to India. We shall bring up our baby here, in England.'

He raises an eyebrow and quizzes.

'Using home brewed beer for our sustenance?'

'No! Any qualified Cambridge graduate can get a job.'

I burbled on with disconnected garbage. Bill's mood changed.

'You're planning my life, eh?'

It was a voice, I didn't recognise; it made me uncomfortable.

'I'll be better tomorrow'.

I let him leave.

Left alone, I entered a dark world. To date, a degree from Cambridge had been my *Primmum mobile*. Would I now have to let it go? Would Bill take care of the three of us? Now, reality dawned in its starkness. Despite regular intimacy, I didn't really know the man. It was the lunacy of falling in love. I screamed, I cried, I horrored, beating my belly as if the baby was at fault. I have sinned; I need to be punished; my entire Lal family will be disgraced. I don't want to live!

Bill returned the next morning. The anger had gone. Gently, he strokes my belly. He lifts my streaming eyes to look into his face. His eyes were warm, a totally changed man from the night before.

'Have you told your parents?'.

'Not yet.'

'I'll do it for you,' he suggests.

It was the one conversation, I dreaded. A fool has rushed in where angels fear to tread. Back in India a rocket would explode. In the world of the fifties such behaviour is anathema, however modern they strive to be.

We made that strategic phone call from a public booth. Bill picked up the receiver and popped in a bunch of shillings.

'I want to marry Prami.' He was direct and to the point. The dart hit bull's eye without need for explanation.

'We are coming over immediately,' was Father's grim reply. He put down the phone. My poppy day antics must have been noticed and relayed back. Even then, I'd crossed the line of decency.

*

I return to Girton to await my parents. Night comes and the same woman finds herself in the same bed regurgitating like the sheep in the next meadow.

It was clear from Bill's probing questions about lifestyle in a rich household that he wanted the pickings for himself. Unwittingly I had loaded him with a dowry. I had opened my mouth too wide and swallowed a fly!

On arrival Father acts very civil towards Bill; one could expect no less from a gentleman. although Mother could hardly meet my face, and as for Bill, even his name freezes in her tongue. It was charged first meeting, a thundercloud that never burst. What's the use? The deed is done; the bed is made; I must now lie on it.

What's for sure, Father wants me to get me married straightaway, though Mother, the more practical one, would have preferred abortion as the sensible option. I don't agree for all life is sacred and Father accepts my wish but for a totally different reason.

However, being a respected figure in his community must retain his status, not stain his image with a sleazy back story. He will announce a new son-in-law with pride, a brilliant scholar from Cambridge, coming from a renowned family.

The very name Le Hunte suggests pedigree and Mother could boast of her new grandchild and receive congratulations from the ladies of Victoria club. As for the child, whenever it arrived, it would be declared as born premature.

A clinical finale to what could have been a happy love story.

We will get married and Prami, the rebel must make vows she's never planned.

A Hindu marriage has been agreed; it's what I wanted, going back to my culture.

Father knows just the man for the job and the right place; the home of his friend in Holland Park, but unfortunately, his floor is fully carpeted and the ceremony requires a sacred fire to bear witness to our vows. Rising to the occasion, puts down kitchen foil held in place by four bricks. He has already collected incense and sandalwood and from a temple in Southall and the bullock cart is readied for the show. In a funny sort of way so am I. Earlier, I had considered the whole scenario of an Indian marriage as being over the top, but watching the set come to life, I come to realise what is happening is not so different from the plays I had directed at St Bede's.

Now, Bill would need a script and stage directions. We both must garland each other with white and red flowers threaded with green mango leaves.

'Call it a symbolic ritual of acceptance of each other'.

'More like opening the stable door after the horse has bolted,' he quips.

As the ceremony progresses, wisps of incense swirl up to the skies.

Seven times we circle the fire, making our marriage vows and asking for health, prosperity and lasting companionship. By the end the power of the moment engulfs me. The covenant is richer than the simpler 'I do' of a Christian ceremony and I'm thankful to Bill that he has behaved well so far. He's an atheist and could well have blown everything off-target with his dry sense of humour.

Finally, the priest asks us to look at the North star, the symbol of eternal steadfastness. A look of amusement crosses Bill's face as he addresses the priest, 'Not so easily done in London, Sir; I wouldn't bet on fair skies.'

The solemn mood has collapses at his uncalled-for intervention. Naturally, everyone is watching him, even Father carries a frown. I must save the day.

'Don't know where the pole star might be, never seen it in Girton. Why not try Hampstead or someplace even further north? Scotland?'

The tension has defused. We all laugh; the party can start. Now, Bill is knocking back the samosas and peeling an alphonso mango. Three cheers!

Round the fire I have taken a journey, so alive, resonant and beautiful; the wild, wild girl has become a married woman.

Is that the road to Everest or is it a stumbling block?

And now, the story of my wedding, a couple of days later.

Imagine a wedding breakfast by the Avon gorge.

Father has brought us to this place for our wedding breakfast, miles away from the robotic civil ceremony that he thought was imperative less Bill try and slip away. The hedges are alive with the sound of summer, a butterfly, resplendent in multi-coloured outfit pays a courtesy call to the gathered guests, and a pigeon does the same his own way, by cooing white splat on a nearby garden path.

Years ago, jogging as a penniless student on the Downs, he had come across this iconic hotel and had promised himself that when he was a man of means, he would return here to this place. And voilà here we are! Mother has brought her billowing sari; she moves among the green lawns in full sail with the wind from river Avon coming from behind her. As for me, I was prepared for the occasion by Mother who has handed over a red sari without a word. Red, by the way is a virgin bride's colour and providing it for me must highlight her insult to a fallen girl. Bill and Father are in suites; the hotel has provided them with carnation buttonholes. And a photographer is wating, for this to be the grand wedding for the Indian public.

We await the arrival of the mother-in law, I'm ready for the bullring.

Elsie Mary Lavinia Le Hunte enters with her neighbour, the doughty Aunty Nell, who Bill likes, and greets her warmly. Doll, as she's known looks ridiculous in her royal blue suit with grossly coloured feathers sculpted on her hat and thick stockings covering her varicose veins: a cartoon character.

We toy with the banquet with barely disguised courtesy. While Father is dribbling with small talk, I stare openly into Doll's eyes without blinking. I've have thrown the gauntlet. Without even starting it, we're at war.

Will she rise to the occasion?

She does.

Elsie Le Hunte rises and snaps her handbag. It is not a toast, but a declaration of war. She announces that she is going to Wales and will take her son to meet his family.

I'm bursting to confront her, but Father pulls me down.

Now ensues a tacit altercation with Aunty Nell vigorously poking her elbow into the puffing Elsie's chest. Pigeons at war! Eventually, a treaty ensues, with a glowered admission by Doll that she will allow her son to return to his wife.

'An excellent decision, Mother. We'll all come to Broad Haven another day.'

Father is graciousness itself and agrees with her as if such a decision is the most natural thing to do, for Bill has family in Wales. He rises to see them off. and tells the photographer he will select the best selection from the proofs.

Alas, there has been no peep out of Bill as his mother fires warning shots for my husband's capture and triumphant removal of him as her prisoner of war. I'm annoyed at Bill's obsequious silence. For God's sake he's the pawn she wishes to control. At this Mad Hatter's Tea Party, he's the mole who sleeps. Ditto at the bottle party. Doll collects her things to leave and marches home.

A little change of direction for us as well. We shall take her suggestion and go off to Wales, minus the lady with the handbag. Bill is chuffed to little NAAFI breaks.

1958

Welcome to Wales
Croeso I Gymru:
Broad Haven, Pembrokeshire,
Land of my Fathers

We hit the road and in no time, find ourselves by the front door of Uncle Len's cottage right by the sea. Even now the sound of the retreating Atlantic, reaches me from the deep distance. Although it's fresh and sunny today, Bill tells me that in winter, the gentle sloping bowl cradling the village with its sheer cliffs on either side vaporises into nothingness, becoming one with the ocean. Little wonderer the ancient Celts believed this place to be the end of the world, for beyond, into the Atlantic, lie coils of mist that roll on and on. From somewhere in the lost beyond, our child will come.

Lost in reverie, I feel a light touch. it's Uncle Len for Bill has gone. He puts out his hand in welcome, and not a word about pregnancy. There's is no acrimony that he wasn't invited, but then everyone knows about Doll and her ways.

Uncle Len is a retired architect distinguished by a slight scar on his lower lip into which he constantly stuffs a pipe, be it dormant or smoking. Did the scar come first, or did the pipe leave a lasting impression? Chicken or egg? No time for silly conjecture. He invites me in, telling me that Bill has already found his way to the beach.

I find Len's parlour more like an over-stuffed museum and tucked away to one side is his brother, Uncle Harry, he's nodding off. Prominent on the mantlepiece is the Le Hunte coat of arms that suggests they may be people of consequence, yet their motto suggests otherwise!

Parcare Prostatitis, meaning, Spare the Vanquished! Who lost, who won over the years? One Le Hunte became Governor of Jamaica, another was hanged. Another Le Hunte was sent by Cromwell to bomb Pembroke Dock that earned him a title and swathes of land across the county that was lost when a latter-day successor spent it all on buying strips of land for a railway line joining England to Ireland. So, even today there must be a long snake-like tract that is Le Hunte territory. We might well be landed gentry of nettles and furrows. A mixed bag these Le Huntes. I'm sure there is a rogue gene working its way down. Prami, be prepared!

Any other signs of royalty? There is a pair of Chinese vases standing at each end of the mantel piece as loyal supporters of the plaque. To be accepted, I must present my own credentials. I inform Uncle Len, about the library of Victoria Cub with portraits on the wall of previous *burrah sahibs* as Presidents. Uncle Len has heard of Victoria Club. I reckon I have passed the litmus test.

'Where did you get these beautiful ornaments?' I ask.

'My father got it back when he returned home after the Chinese Boxer rebellion where he served in the Royal Navy as a boilerman.'

I have a sneaky feeling he might have pilfered them. Vases do not bloom on machinery. I'm drawn to Uncle Len despite him being a leftover of some past glory. I was beginning to wonder whether I had accidentally conveyed to Bill that the Lal family was also of impeccable descent when I twittered away about dowries. There is a rustle from the kitchen.

'Hello!'

In comes Aunty Glad of the great hug and the big smile, as roly-poly as a pudding. That's the kind of Le Hunte I like, natural and genuine, not the woman with the painted bird on her hat. She almost knocks a vase down as she hugs me; I straighten this valuable heirloom as Aunt gets busy with some dusting. I'm sure she wants to overhear. We carry on our conversation on the Boxer rebellion, how they targeted the white missionaries for bringing in a foreign culture in their midst. I do a double-take. Am I the foreign culture in question?

Aunt hasn't taken in a word of our conversation; a speck on the table is calling for attention. In any case she knows nothing of boxers, nor is interested. It's flannel underwear for her husband.

She pops a Welsh cake into her mouth.

'I don't hold with fasting,' she insists, 'You only get cut up.'

She passes the rest to us and bustles out wiping her hands on the edge of her apron in readiness for setting the table. Would you believe it, this lady has entered marriage with false teeth as dowry, for then there'll be no further charge on her husband? Instead, a permanent white smile.

'Dinner will be on the table in two minutes. All of you to the mackerel; I've soused it all night.'

'Aye,' responds Uncle Harry from the window where his eyes have been staring into middle distance; he has his own pipe dreams.

For me he holds a curious interest for I have learnt from Bill he's trying to invent a perpetual motion machine in his garage, and he'll give the patent to his nephews! And then, boyo, we shall all become rich! What an endearing loving family!

It's good to see Bill amongst his own people. Would he like to end up a Pembrokeshire man so strong seems to be the pull of the place? I wouldn't mind bringing up a child here. Unfortunately, Bill has other ideas and it is Prami who has put them there with all this jazz about life in exotica. *Mea culpa*.

During dinner, Aunt points beyond the bowl of hills and tells me to ask Bill to take me to Prescelly mountain. It has acres of grassy hillside dotted about with little white lambs frolicking with their mums. She winks at me, clearly a hint about the baby. An embarrassed Uncle Len tries to hush her; he's is too much of a conservative for such a carry-on, but Aunt can't contain herself, so more frolicking lambs till she runs out of breath. Poor lady, they have no children of their own so a baby would be welcome and both of them could frolic with the lambs. But can a roly-poly frolic? I try to stifle a giggle as Uncle Harry brings in a jug of home-brewed beer.

So, it's bottoms up with home-brew and farewell to the lambs. Iechyd da!

Next morning, Aunt wakes me up with a cool glass of elderflower pop and preps me for the day. She has taken charge, this lovely lady.

'Prami, get Bill to take you for a walk each morning. Climb to the top of Prescelly mountain and you can see the whole world.'

It's strange to think that even though they knew America was on the other side, Pembrokeshire, folk look inwards for their universe. However, this time, narrowing down the universe to Broad Haven, she suggests I take a walk along the front to pick up some Welsh bacon from Mock's shop along the front.

'There's nothing like a piece of Welsh bacon,' adds Uncle Harry from his window and he's been around the world while Aunt is firmly rooted in Pembrokeshire in a village where one has to put out a hand to stop the train.

'Will you join me, Uncle Len?'

'Aye,' responds Len. 'It's such a perfect day. We'll let Prami take it easy and enjoy a feast of Australia from Unc and I'll catch up with you.'

Bill leaps off the chair with energy I've never noticed before.

'Maybe, Aunt will teach Prami some baking,' he laughs. 'I could do with some more Welsh cakes.'

Bill's a very likeable man amongst his own tribe. I'm reminded of the man who won me over with his stories of Broad Haven. I'm watching the pair strolling happily down the seafront.

The long sandy expanse in front has filled with trippers who unpack their cars with so much paraphernalia that I wonder how it would ever go back. Soon, they will be starting the priority of white man getting brown, while their children explore more innocent pleasures like wading with their little shrimp catching nets into little rock pools the tide has left behind. I can see on my right some boys trying to clamber up the majestic lion rock where the monarch stares balefully into the sea and gaping behind him are dark, cavernous granite caves hiding secrets that one must discover.

I feel a nudge. It's Aunt; she winks at me again.

'I'm back to clean up the kitchen and that takes a long time.'

She obviously wants to leave me with Uncle Harry to allow him time to dig out more information about me for she has never met an Indian before and I for one, want to find out more about Uncle Harry. From what Bill has told me of his past, he intrigues me; he's a frontier man like Father.

He looks so out of place in this Chinese elegance with his three-piece buttoned-up suit and farmer's boots. He's still, staring into middle distance. If I don't start a conversation, he'll be soon asleep but Aunt hasn't left.

She seems totally absorbed cleaning a grainy black and white photograph of the couple that is hanging on the wall. It has been taken on a beach on a hot summer's day and Harry is in the same outfit that he's wearing today and beside him, his wife in a dress that looks a different length right to left. They seem to be holding hands.

'How old was Unc then?' I ask the Derby and Joan couple.

'An easy sixty,' she replies with her beaming smile, 'Let him tell you about Australia and the black fella.' I'm shocked at her choice of words; my convent education prevents me from smiling back, yet I'm delighted that this might well be her exit speech that allows Uncle Harry to start his story.

'When I reached Australia, I jumped ship in Sydney,' started Harry. Some old people begin their stories from the middle.

'Jumped ship?' My ears are alert; here's an interesting man.

'I teamed up with a black fella…'

Ah! That's what he called his partner.

My imagination flares up as he carries on his disjointed sequence in broken phrases like Father. Harry went not just to dig for gold, but trusting his Celtic sixth sense, to 'divine' it!

Onward and onward, he follows the aborigine, a forked stick in each hand.

One momentous day, the stick quivers and shudders, and falls to the ground. He knows in his heart that he's standing on pay dirt; a rock glints, catching the sun. He picks up the stone, takes it to the top of the ridge and holds it to direct sunlight.

'Welcome Friend!' He can now stake a claim for riches are his for the asking.

Ah! that's why Aunt winked, wanting me to find out where this gold is hidden? She could do with some gold for Harry's only job is taking care of the bicycle sheds at a nearby air force base, RAF Brawdy.

I keep munching Aunt's cakes as Harry talks Perhaps, it's the baby! As I sneak into the umbilical, Unc is still as Harry moving along with his story.

Amidst the excitement of the find, there comes to 'Arry' as Aunt calls him, one of those crucial pauses for thought that bookmark our lives. He remembers a host of rough prospectors, some are earlier mates, who had found gold and, with single-minded intent, they burnt up their lives in the bars and brothels of Sydney. The sermons of preachers he has so conveniently ignored, sound a whisper, then a warning, then a command.

He throws away the rock, and armed with a self-generated platitude, that it's better to think he's found gold, then to discover there was nothing there, he returns home. There is no sense of disappointment or regret. Now he's looking for perpetual motion; He's both philosopher, engineer and visionary, all rolled into one. He's is on the road to Everest himself.

These good people are now my new family, along with Aunty Herbert who became family long ago. Three cheers to Prami's army. It marched along with me for many years till more frolicking lambs were added. Any roadblocks? Just chicken pox.

'I've got the bloody chicken pox', sang the baby sopranos and their voices carried over to Mock's shop.

1960

Cambridge: Nurse Binodni

Returning from Wales after this momentous first introduction I find Father has been busy; with great foresight he has used his missionary contacts and arranged for a tribal nurse to be brought over. With missionaries and their tribal conversions, you win some, you lose some, for many are deep in the jungle, and fortunately, out of their radar. Jesus is not the best fisherman in Mosaboni. I hope this one turns out good.

When my Father fetches Binodni from Heathrow, it's like a wish come true. She looks familiar with the typical tribal face, dark skin, broad nose and crinkly hair that I had seen in the Santhals that worked as Mother's domestic staff. Mother would call her *'junglee'*.

Binodni arrives eager to swing into action, eager to help, eager to learn about England. We chat away whetting her enthusiasm, especially Bill who has never come across a tribal person before. He had thought the Welsh were tribal enough, but this hybrid of country mouse and town mouse is in a class by herself, living in a doomed world dominated by Satan and Calcutta. She has turned out to be a Jehovah's witness.

As all roads lead to Rome all conversation heads for Calcutta, her Mecca of dreams.

The storyteller within me is awake. I wish to entertain her on her first day. I know where come from and I know what they want; festivals and bazaars with plenty of money to spend. I start with the great annual festival of Durga Pooja in Calcutta, how the goddess comes down from the Himalayas to save mankind. She's a beautiful woman, riding a tiger and has many arms each carrying a weapon for defeating the demons.

Binodni cuts me short with a scream.

'You are talking about the Devil! Get me out of this place quickly!'

I had forgotten she was sourced from Father's missionary connections. She is a Jehovah's Witness.

She tries to escape, but Father catches her on the run.

'No Binodni, no! Your elders have confirmed there is no devil in Cambridge and I've have taken their permission before bringing you here.'

Father may have calmed her fears, but I was wrong- footed from the start. Would she ever trust me Nevertheless, she was excellent domestic support and Bill enjoyed her company but she would have none of it. Always high-strung, she interprets his simple handshake as fondling and looking at her with a smile as blatant lust.

Bill treats it as a laugh; he's simply baiting her for fun. It's that insouciant smile that he cannot handle.

Then it's my turn to yet again make another stupid mistake. *En passant* I mention to her that some women come to England to catch a British husband and make a match of it. I was only trying to flatter her striking looks, not offering my husband.

Somehow, this nested in her mind.

When winter arrives with its dark days, culture shock impacts like a hammer. She starts to believe that marriage was the reason I'd brought her to England and insists on meeting a potential white husband! She's was totally disenchanted with Bill, who in her strained imagination rejected her after first showing interest.

She also hates me as a scheming bitch for enticing her under false pretences. Obviously, I'm a child of Satan.

Grey cell by grey cell she's growing mad before my eyes, though Bill finds her eccentric and amusing.

When the winter weather was forgiving, she takes solitary walks in nearby Parker's Peace where she can hear Bill's mocking laughter resounding all around and naked trees mocking her with insidious tease.

'Jehovah has abandoned me!' she laments, over and over again! Her eyes become distraught and wild. She spreads out her frizzy hair and shakes it about, looking every inch a witch. Enough was enough; we searched for some kind of Jehovah's Witness support group, but none was around. One morning, I catch her stroking a bread knife. To welcome the new baby, or kill me? My time has almost come and both parents have returned.

In desperation, I demand of Father,
'Kick her out of here this minute!'

All through the train ride to London, she transforms into a drama queen who is being forced unwillingly by this old man into some loony bin. She now truly believes this is the case, and with cunning magnifies the role for the watching passengers. Father is in danger of being reported to the authorities; he tries to calm them by explaining that this poor woman has just received really bad news from home and begged their patience.

When Binodni recognises Heathrow from where she had arrived, and not the loony bin as her destination, she lets out a big whoop and bolts like a runaway horse, pushing aside the waiting passengers. With a resounding, Halleluiah, she's on her way to Jehovah!

But to tell the truth, Father has booked her a ticket to Calcutta.

'If we ever make it to Calcutta,' remarks Bill, 'I could ask her to fetch me a juicy Bengali virgin.'

No, it was not a throwaway tease, perhaps, a bit of a threat. Sudden shudder within me as if someone had walked over my grave.

1960

Cambridge:
7 months later

A cold winter preceded the 'arrival'. As March winds blew, a baby comes to life, tapping away at will. When delicate and tickling, she's a ballerina, when punching, he's a boxer. Bill would like a boy. His dynastic impulse is uppermost.

As I walk round my little flat with its pillared hall, I feel grandiose in my bulging belly. I find a kind of inner settlement, call it contentment. I'm the first woman in the Garden of Eden, bearing the first child of Creation. I put Bill's hand on my moving belly.

'Just feel, the baby's moving.'

The baby never answers; with its little kicks and gyrations, it's dancing with the Santhals. I want Bill to stroke the awakening baby, share my excitement at a brave new world, but Bill simply rolls over, pulls up the covers with an explicit warning.

> *'Poor Tom's a-cold.'*
> Shakespeare: *King Lear*

His wish list is transparent. As the sap rises the mercury falls. Whatever sex I permitted had dwindles in proportion to my rising belly. A time comes when the barometer freezes and poor little Tom was left out in the cold. That's the barometer of life.

However, his hormones 'hotted' up as soon as he learnt that he'd fathered a boy. What conjugal bliss to follow; Tom's ready for the plunge but life never works that way.

After the birth, complications with the stiches got me infected. It took time to heal and Tom's back in the cold as the as the March winds sweep from the fens.

Bill gets frustrated at my fumbling attempt to satisfy and speaks out with anger that he can barely conceal.

'Other girls do it instinctively, but you seem to know nothing at all.

How dare he expect more? Kama Sutra is not in the shelves of the colonel's library. Did I marry a womaniser? Three extant girlfriends at our first meeting must only be the tip of the iceberg? I must escape from this man.

However, I've never been one for confrontation. To act as injured party would have put premium on his accomplished tongue. Rationalisation seems the only way to lick my wounds. I'm rightly my own person, a soul not a hole. I shall make my own way.

Quo Vadis, Prami? Remember Mary has a little lamb. How can you leave little Baa-Baa behind?

Of course, I can't, but I can stay clear of the shepherd.

There is plenty around that nibble the field; he can be a bad shepherd and rustle from another's flock.

Meanwhile, I'll tend to my tank a mini-world of my own. Freud would call it sublimation.

In my excitement, when we moved into our first home, we'd had gone to Market Square and chose, a panorama of fish with the same care one would design a summer garden: rainbow guppies that have carried their variegated colour from the sky, wag their tails like little propellers; an orange swordfish and with its piercing black tail as long as its body, defends his kingdom; it can leap out of water and strike the enemy, charging backwards. The orange tiger barb, burning bright, hunts among the green swaying grass that forms the forest of our realm. Come night the shoal of neon tetras will sprinkle the aquarium with fairy lights. My flagship angel with her silver sails will journey majestically across the fish frontier, telling all mankind, 'It's Christmas!' and our little flat is ready for the birth.

A storm preceded the baby's arrival, but his birth on the Ides of March, a day of warning for Julius Caesar, was for me the dawning of the sun. As I stared at the infant tucked away in his soft little swaddling, aeons of time slip by; the child becomes a man who I will name Arjun, the first person in the *Gita* allowed to see the face of God.

A little 'miracle' also happened in the aquarium; a guppy gave birth to several fry. Coincidence or congratulations from above? Bill sent me a card to the maternity hospital, very sweet, but mainly about the fry! He's not a man who wears his heart on his sleeve, but he did admit that I looked very desirable while nursing the baby. I shall have to be content with that single admission, maybe of love, or more probably for the little Le Hunte he had planned to create. He will be a good father to him.

Managing the baby turns out to be fun. The midwife steps in and teaches Bill how to 'top and tail' the baby during his bath, and he performs it with such style that the infant gurgles as water dribbles down his side. There ae more than one way to capture love. Could it be the wriggly way?

The pair look like Porky and Pig, as tiny Arjun sits on daddy's lap getting his hair tumbled with a soft towel. He dries the infant with his own adaptation of Schubert's Trout Quintet, very juicy in nature.

> 'My fruit's an apricot.'
> *Fruitee is an apricot.*

The tune is catchy and momentum builds up till Bill, lying on the bed, raises the infant in the air. Voila! Jubilation and orchestration all in one.

What a tale to tell his children, 'Granddad thought you were an apricot!' Bill would never live it down. This is married life at its best. I have put aside the past.

We even change paddy pads together, making a game of it.

> *'Knick Knack Paddywhack give a dog a bone;*
> *this little boy comes rolling home.'*

Bill is enchanted with the latest Le Hunte. Give the dog his bone and let him wag his tail.

*

Final exams came and went, and different *au pairs* also came and chased by testosteronic students they shuffled in the spare room and slid away secretly as bats of night.

Bill was amused at their shenanigans and told me to keep away; 'Let the dog have his day. Why get worked up for what you can't see?'

What if you can? When we return to the flat one evening, we find a man, *in flagrante* on a sofa with our German *au pair*. After the first shock comes the revelation. Naked, he's a stunningly desirable with a physique of a wrestler.

He makes not the slightest effort to cover himself as he rises, and my eyes beam in on the right places with rising passion. Startled at myself, I retract my give-away glances with snap of an eyelid. In their place I attach a deeply carved frown, insist he respect an Indian lady and her home. My melodrama of righteous indignation doesn't work; this man won't budge, he pulls up his trouser zip very slowly, he tosses away my supposed anger with a quizzical raised eyebrow.

'What's wrong with a little poking between friends?'

He raises an eyebrow with meaning and questions with his eye. I chuck him out. All happens in a jiffy, but Bill, watching me closely, comes to his own conclusion. What will happen in our bed tonight?'

He tried to rape me in his anger, and I had to fight him off. The first time Bill laid his hands on me.

Soon graduation is over, the May balls are over and the steel bands scattered in college courtyards now silent; banarama rum cocktails are drained to the last drop, madrigals on the river are a memory; parting tears for friendships, formed over three years, cast a shade of tristesse.

We'll set off to India where Father has booked us a first-class cabin in P&O's latest liner, *Himalaya*. He has promised me a holiday in India. What I didn't realise at the time was that it was also a ploy for total management of my new husband who he assessed as a *fly-by-night lover*, and would pin him down. The truth is clear, I'd really not escaped at all.

*

Time has come to say goodbye to my tutor and Girton. I've hardly been there since my marriage, but I know, for a fact that she came to the rescue arranging for a change of subject from English to Social Anthropology after learning from Father that I grew up amidst tribal people. Less reading needed in that case, less pressure. Throughout the years in Cambridge, I never suspected the humanity within.

Am I sorry to leave Cambridge? When reaching the summit of my ambition, I had felt like Tiger Tenzing planting a flag on Everest and despite a roller-coaster marriage, my Raleigh bike still peddles fine; I've kept up momentum from the day I started my journey, from the day, the beetle set off on a tram.

1960

Choppy Waters of the Ocean

After the austerity of nine terms of student life a luxurious fortnight on the ocean waves feels like heaven in a P&O liner.

The highlight of the journey is the passage through the Suez Canal; the channel is so narrow that even passing camels can wave and so can boisterous little pharaohs who have gone wild; there's camaraderie between ship and desert. The moment the ship docks at Alexandria, Egyptian vendors gather round in little boats with leather camels and rugs. An old man at the end of the boat squats with a hookah, loaded with the heady mixture of tobacco and molasses that he breathes into his nostrils with the hubble-bubble sound at each intake It's fiery hot as the sun glazes the desert, making sweet red bottles of sherbet, a must-have cholera beverage. I try and stop Bill nibbling at fly-garnished bowls of raisins and nuts, but all is grist when all are pissed. Bill haggles to perfection and we buy a camel that will rock'n'roll in the Arabian Sea, but the infant is neither amused, nor entertained by this visitor; at three months, mother's breast is a much better seduction.

My man is tanning; he reminds me of some Nordic God, released from Valhalla, languorous and handsome. His hair is bleached even further from basking in the tropical sun; his arcane *je-ne-sais-quoi* charm draws in women of all sorts, brown, white, and black in swimming costumes and bikinis, doing what the orient does best, massaging the old boy to rampancy. As his fan club gains momentum, it's obvious he doesn't need me. It's a motley female-studded holiday, while a cobra watches, ready to spit.

It's going to be a hard slog to get him back; but, will I even try? Let's see.

There's going to be the usual fancy dress contest tonight with guests parading in the seductive and the bizarre. No challenge for the brain behind Poppy Day. Finding inspiration from the Suez, Cleopatra emerges as the clear favourite, making her mortal yearnings more palpable by an emerging rubber snake, peering from her cleavage.

Predicting riotous behaviour at the party that will follow, I use Bill's dirty old sock, the dirtier the better, and my white headband to model him as 'sock in the eye', for that's what he deserves. Any passion has gone, but on the deck, I notice the pennant flies high. There's life in the old boy yet. I'll use it to test myself if I still care.

Once downstairs, I use my wherewithal to hang on to Bill. I taunt and tease with the Cleopatra adder as Bill chases me round our little cabin like an out-of-control school boy.

Instinctively, I 'done' something right. With a hardened heart, I accept the conclusion: this is a marriage based on sex.

This is the house that Prami built; its mortgage paid with sex. Can I keep it up?

Our supposed holiday is heading to Barbil which is the present headquarters for Father's mining operations' He tells me it will be just as good as Mosaboni but I know nothing will.

1960-1962

Bombay:
Back home at last

We had to first dock in Bombay. Celebrations ahoy! After throwing out the Portuguese imperialist in Goa, the entire Indian Navy was moored alongside, their ships loaded with booze for the Portuguese had made Goa a free port and flooded their little state with imported booze. Naturally, Father who has to have connections everywhere, seems to know some officers in the flagship, so parties galore! Bill could surf it on imported booze as happy as a sand boy on the beach. But why this benevolence? Why this diversion in the road map? I thought Father wanted the falcon to be kept hooded. Best to keep Bill under his nose but falcons are birds of prey and the predator had no problem swooping down for quality red meat available in the gilded cages in Grant Road where fully juiced women lean over balconies, their breasts sticking out, saris undone, with promise of manna on the second floor. I look away. As you may have realised already, my ignorance of manna is acute, but men will be men.

It is still not clear why Father created this pit stop. Slowly it dawns that he is a theatre director himself with a cute mind. He had planned the plot down to the last scene.

He had found a job for Bill with a British waterproofing company, called, Gladstone & Lyle; he knew the chairman and persuaded him to take on Bill.

Our holiday dragged on for another year and so it came to pass that Bill climbed ladders to rooftops, and I made babies. Although Bill is no great lover yet we keep popping them out, so we must be doing something right.

I remember, the dramatic birth of my premature twin daughters. I was in an exclusive nursing home paid for by the company when the when the heavens opened.

'Doctor, doctor, quickly, quickly! Come immediately to room 1', cries a nurse.

'Madam's baby is coming!' I hear footsteps racing down the corridor, and being loaded like cargo entering a ship. The rest is blankety-blank. I open my eyes. Can't hear any baby, just nurses calling out, 'Look. what you've got! Two little baby girls.'

'Can I see them?'

I ask no one in particular, and a nurse is about to comply when the doctor shouts, 'Stop, they must go immediately to intensive care.'

She wouldn't even allow me touch them. If only I could have fondled them, felt their little cheeks, whispered my love, our life together would have turned out different.

I'm left with sorrow for the precious moments that were denied. What if I was allowed to fondle my babies, hug them with love?

So many 'what ifs' in life, Prami. Don't make an excuse for this one. You simply handed them over to Mother and she was delighted to take charge. What if you had been a better mother and stayed at home. All you wanted to do was party with Bill. You're fast becoming an alcoholic. Excuses, Excuses, ostrich dear!'

When the monsoons came. Bill got sacked for deserting his team. I think that's exactly what Father was waiting for, just how long Bill would last. We are now ready for Barbil.

1962-1965

Barbil:
The Young Family

Barbil turned out totally different from my ringlet days in Mosaboni. The rumbustious hideout of the British club has gone with Christmas father. arriving in a humble jeep with billy goats as escort. Instead, the place is overrun with lorries and Lambrettas as big money pushes in. Yet it still bears the footprint of our nearby mines, the dusty carpet of red earth is corrugated by passing lorries rich with iron ore. and local pie dogs chase China Dodge lorries with five-star barking.

It's the rainy season. A huge clap of thunder unleashes the power of the monsoons. Sheets of lightning drawn magnetically by the iron ore in the soil, flash with regular strobes as arrows of rain force their way through the side of the jeep. The river Karo is flooded and gathering momentum at a dangerous rate as the red earth of the hillside sweeps down upon its waters.

Most days, Karo is a sweet little stream from where women fetch water on their heads in large earthen jars but I'm told that in full pelt it can even sweep a fully loaded lorry! But the driver knows her moods; he scans the grey, granite stones jutting outwards, gauges the depth of the water, puts the jeep into four-wheel drive and pushes us safely through the torrent,

We pass the compound of the Figredos, Anglo-Indian, friends of Father. A guard at the gate of their compound waves to us; he is awaiting our arrival, has seen the smoky puff-puff from the locomotive.

It will be a pell-mell event when it arrives: heralded by the engine sounding off as it passes the nearest level crossing, a cue for venders to jump to action.

'Look, here comes the rail *gari*!'

The *chai garam* man gets his large aluminium kettle of hot tea ready to pour into thimble size clay pots; folk who have arrived from distant villages, roll-up their make-shift bedding and wipe snot from the children's noses; a lame beggar adjusts his crutches and he's off full pelt towards the mark where the first-class carriage stops. Bounty has come to town. Mangoes may drop out from baskets 'Marie' biscuits will spill ending up as crumbled offerings for local pie dogs, and any white man emerging will be pick-pocketed.

We pass dense jungles on either side. One day, I tell him we'll go for a night ride and see the mighty bison in the spotlight, their brown hump-backs silhouetted against the moonlight, white socks like footballers, eyes staring at our spotlight, with the nightjar always waiting on the road, the porcupine scurrying in ungainly escape, its spears glinting in the headlights, sambhar deer with his huge horns staring from the bushes, and a leopard perhaps, lying in wait for a hunt.

Bill is not too interested in my jungle; his eyes are seeking the novelty of the scenes unfolding around him. He's a come-alive tourist absorbing rural India.

As we rumble through the ramshackle buildings of Barbil, Bill compares it to a typical outpost from a western movie, complete with dusty traffic and a sleepy sheriff passing time with local women in topless saris. His eyes pop at the local talent as a passing lorry laden with iron ore and female labour covers his shirt in red dust.

It's best to introduce the chorus line right from the start; they are one singular, topless sensation, balancing and swaying high on top with iron ore lorries as their stage. It's the can-can all over again. I'm sure Bill has made a mental note of a season ticket. He notes me watching and tries to distract.

'Show me *The Good, the Bad and the Ugly*,' he commands with see-through enthusiasm, trying to look like a boy lining up at the cinema for a 'Western' on a Saturday afternoon.

'And, where's the boozer?' he enquires.

'Well, my dear husband,' I tell the lotus eater with a bite in my voice, 'it has to be the director's bungalow especially designated for your Royal Highness. See the labour huttings ahead, circling the perimeter like a ragged fringe on a petticoat?'

'You are obsessed with petticoats,' he teases ignoring the sarcasm.

I remind him, 'Why not, it's the route your hands took at the Girton Ball!'

We break into spontaneous laughter. A little ribaldry at last! It's revealing to note how pleased Bill feels in Lotus land. The company staff is gathered to garland us with marigolds, the women having to get on their toes to reach the upright '*Burra Sahib*' Arjun is passed round like a parcel with hyperbole laid on in Oriya and at every transfer his cheeks pinched by the women.

'May you have long life as maharajah of the mines. And may God pour his bounty on the little *sahib*.' The little sahib in question wanted none of this bounty pushed into his mouth. He howled and stretched out his arms to me. I have kept the twins safely in the jeep because they are still delicate and prone to germs.

Bill soaks in the adulation. The manager steps forward and gives Bill a bunch of pink floribunda roses with a low *namaste*. I didn't hear much more of his convoluted welcome speech, the sound of clapping and the thump, thump, thump of the Santhal drummers had taken over.

They dragged Bill to dance with them on the dusty road.

'We give you welcome, Sir *sahib*,' and the rest of staff, *salaamed* as if to an inspecting general and Bill obliged, thumping with two left feet out of sync with the beating drums.

And I wondered what the hell was going on. Just at that moment a short man in a white turban with a belt cummerbund in the middle stepped forward and *salaamed*.

Welcome also to Nalda club, *bare sahib* we are having

party tonight because we are beginning the Lions club of Barbil, everyone that matters will be there. Why don't you become our lion tamer?

A hearty boost to his ego but a punch in the middle for me. Would you believe it, wives of members are known as lionade? Poxy lemonade? Fie!

And so, Bill settled into his job; morning trips to inspect the mines surrounded by obsequious staff, and possible screening of female labour thereafter. Grant Road all over again but, but this time without Prami. The finale was buttered rum at Nalda club where we became members. He was satisfied but I was not. I wanted more from marriage. Any love life we had was becoming routine, 'Whip it in, whip it out and wipe it', as if he was washing dishes in a hurry. How debasing.

Oh, where are the poppy fields of Cambridge where we laughed, where we strolled and got to know each other? This dreadful routine, was it practice at shadow boxing for greater stamina? Bill often came home exhausted from work. I could have crossed my legs, but the Kraken wakes, when poor Tom's a-cold. I'm still fond of the man though a little bit frightened of his dark undercurrents.

However, being young, I can bounce back despite Mother's raids into my family. She dropped in far too frequently and commandeered the twins. Arjun, she usually left in my care and that's great for I still have a family.

He now showing signs of turning into a jungle person like me with a tailful of genes ready to wag.

Like me, Arjun's a fish enthusiast with his own

aquarium of guppies. At his birth some fry is born, and on his fourth birthday, they appear again on a birthday cake. Something Buddhist about that.

From me comes his passion for animals; we now have a monkey as well, cheeky bugger. He makes a nuisance of himself in the village, pinching garments hung out to dry. He jibbers to the twins like a pedagogue, demonstrating the skills of peanut snatching; he urges simian conversation but they cannot speak as yet. Their serious scanning of his antics behoves two scientist-in waiting. Hey! Do not forget the green parrot in a cage that shortly taught the twins to speak after hours and hours of sojourn on potty thrones, with only him for company their first word squawked out a guttural, 'Allo!' Well, one has to start somewhere and parrot-speak will do.

In a matter of weeks Bem will come. As she was conceived in a domestic tempest, she wanted no traffic with this wicked world, and took her time to appear. She's

a joy, and come the time 'lound the 'lagged 'locks, the 'lugged lascal will lun.

For three years she may not be able to pronounce her 'Rs', but evely thing else will be all light.

Meanwhile to urgent matters of the day, Arjun's fourth birthday is upon us where an elephant has been invited as chief guest. Mr Jumbo was first to be served; he finished off our three banana trees. As if this menagerie was not enough, my parents brought in from Calcutta, a bespoke chocolate train, each carriage packed with marzipan zoo animals, though one was replete with guppy. The animals fascinated the twins; they had never been to the zoo. Anju, my older twin daughter gets hold of the giraffe's neck and Ashi topples the zebra in wanton display of some primeval gene. They may not talk yet, but boy, oh boy aren't the twins active?

I have also brought over my mother-in-law from Bristol, encouraging her to meet her grandchildren. but to tell the truth, I wanted her see her son sitting enthroned on a massive wicker chair, the King of the Jungle. She has agreed with no great enthusiasm, but insisted she brings her youngest son, George as well, as he has just finished school. At least George can enjoy the real birds in the forest, not just the dead ones in his mother's hat. Does a hint of a cat come through?

'Have I not done well by your son?' I boast when they arrive. The most she would admit was dismissive.

'He has gone too brown.'

'Aren't you enjoying your new family?'

'The twins are Turks!' she shrieked. No more need be said.

Racist lady, go home, and the likes of you;

I'm the only daughter-in-law you have whose duty demands care and commitment even though my reason as you know was less dutiful.

However, the value-added bonus of their arrival has been the knowledge of Bill the boy, Bill the teenager that has been filled in during after-dinner conversation. Her son seems a shy child, won't answer the telephone refuses to go to church with the family on Sundays. The mother pats her own back at her resourcefulness. Bill could dally with the Sunday joint in the oven while she dallied with the Almighty. Only she didn't quite put it that way. Her warm memories temper my angst at her son's recent behaviour. He was a good lad, once.

The party I planned with end with Arjun's presentation of the jungle; he will take centre stage.

'Stand up at the back, hold firmly to the jeep, pan the spotlight into the forest as far as it will go, and FOCUS. Green eyes mean deer, red eyes mean panther.

He puts his hands to his lips, 'No one must speak.' He lowers his voice. 'You don't know who is listening.' His grandma is on the edge of her seat.

'Do you allow him to go on these dreadful excursions?' she cries out, her eyes firmly fixed on me.

Don't you go with them George', she commands. Bill is a monkey himself. Instead of pouring oil on troubled waters, he ignites them.

'And don't forget the elephants, Baba.' Enough was enough. Doll makes a bee line for the door Father rushes out too, trying to calm the honoured guest. Arjun is disappointed,

'I didn't get time to tell them we were poaching.'

The corner heaved; a gasp chocked the air. In the unscripted exeat, we had forgotten Mother!

I find myself in the cross-hairs of her glare. She focussed on me unblinking and like a judge ready to convict, she spat out her judgment, 'Your son is a *junglee*; he must be punished.'

No, no, he's simply a Noble Savage; he needs to be educated. And I have the right answer. It's a Eureka moment.

Karo Valley School

'Free the child's potential, and you will transform him into the world.'
Maria Montessori

In a place like Barbil, nature will feed the soul, but who will take on this free-ranging son of mine? A school is needed to nourish the mind of the next generation and get it fighting fit for the India of tomorrow. In the old days of the Herberts, the Brits sent their growing children 'back home'. I'm unwilling to send mine away. They are too young. What they need is a trained English teacher, sari girded for the job and yours truly is just the right woman candidate.

Needs joggle cheek by jowl yet there are no English medium schools and we're heading towards a global world. This eastern outpost draws in specialists of every sort. It throngs with engineers and their corporate bosses, accountants fudging books, surveyors searching dense jungles for seams of iron ore, police officers getting richer by the dozen, government administrators with open palms. It's not the leisurely Mosaboni I knew. It's a mini-world of Breughel in action.

I tell myself, Prami, you're a qualified teacher, time to ring another bell. Your son will soon need a school. I shall build a little school for him as well as for these motley people. I overflow with enthusiasm as if building this school would change the world, but it would certainly change mine, take me away from being dragged down by Bill and put me on the map.

'Don't try and make a hero of yourself, Prami, it's just a little school. Simply imagine a space, a line of whitewashed staff quarters. Now, add an ayah, carpenter and plumber, and you have a school. As easy as that. I run it for you and you get busy with your little greying cells.'

I didn't like Bill's tone, being boss has gone to his head.

'And give it a name, Prami, he continues, sardonic and superior. 'Academy for the Polite and the Powerful. You be the polite, simpering head teacher and I shall be the powerful man behind the desk who collects fees.'

'Power to your elbow, eh? But I have a better name for my school' I prefer to name it Karo Valley School after river that flows by the town'

'Grand name, tiny stream.'

I ignore him. I have priorities in my mind. First, I must look for a site. Figerado's empty house would serve the bill. The Anglo-Indian family has migrated to Canada; most Anglo-Indians left the country after the departure of the British. 'Home' became somewhere else for them.

My head starts buzzing; what next? A principal for the school, but who on earth would like to work in the sticks?

A peer, from St. Bede's, responds to my ad in the national papers. She's a lively little person, crisp and firm with an authoritative twinkle. Les, her husband matches her as a 'little man consort'. She takes up the post of headmistress, bringing along husband and five children! For me, where there's a will, there's a way; for her, where there's a need, a way will be found! As for food, local dal and home-grown rice will do nicely.

I also have staff. A Jesuit priest with five tribal offspring tucked away in some hidden village has time on his hands. The Jesuit was previously commandeered by the senior Figerado to celebrate Mass in her house every month, so the school could become a more inviting pit stop for a Formula 1 monk. Many miles along the primrose path though he be, nevertheless he's an antic-laden footballer, rather like a monkey really. And his lessons burst with humour for his domestic experience has made him a past-master of local dialects. He is known for a man of culture. There are rumours he has a room where every wall is covered with books. Naturally, brings us his library, and inevitably, it is all Perry Mason, if you call that culture, but certainly good enough for Bill.

Now Bill has a western friend. Last but not least, my staff is enhanced by an Anglo-Indian lady, Mrs Donald. She has not emigrated to Australia with her children as she failed the colour test for Australia. The country runs a strict 'White Australia' policy; it's a requirement for future settlers to present themselves before an immigration officer and have the colour of their skin examined. Poor Mrs Donald did not qualify and the family left without her; Australia's loss, was my gain.

On the first term she presented a home-grown show of Cinderella that the twins and I watch. Little Arjun appears from the back verandah stage, not holding a slipper but a teddy bear on the cushion, which one of the twins tries to grab.

She conducts a concert every year with her peanut song, 'found a peanut, found a peanut, found a peanut just now' set to 'Oh, my darling Clementine.'

It's a dramatic little piece where the peanut turns out rotten but all is well in the end.

> *'Doctor said I'll live, doctor said I'll live, doctor said I'll live just now.'*
> Traditional

The school will live as the doctor has predicted Whence, thither? How long is a piece of string?

Bill never attended the peanut play, taking no interest in my so-called prancing, but then, neither was I too interested with his club life. At least, there he would find himself centre stage as there's hardly any white man left to play the lead. He might roll out a welcome greeting to a new arrival.

'This is Pramila Le Hunte, my wife. Next time, I'll bring my son and persuade his mother not to leave him at home.'

A not-so-subtle tug-of-war had clearly started for superiority. With well carved niggles he tries put me in place. As long as his Lordship confines himself to the Nalda club; I would let him go ahead with his spin. It has now become a habit.

Little did I know, at the time we arrived, that Father had already alerted the staff that he was sending his son-in-law to oversee the mines, but deliberately did not designate him their manager. He was to be known as Administrative Officer. That got on Bill's wick throughout those four years, for his coronation would be never be complete while I sallied along as S. Lal's daughter.

Just now I don't give a damn how he behaves for my mind is elsewhere; there's an emergency in my country not all that far from Everest.

1964

The Chinese Invasion

*'Hindi-Chini Bhai-Bhai' (Indians and Chinese people
are brothers)*
Popular slogan of the time

While western eyes focussed on Cuba, China invades India from the 'Roof of the World', the snow-covered Himalayas, with their peaks glinting in the sun the like mica, but now infected with Chinese troops in sheer numbers like a plague of locusts. Raiders of the Lost Ark who made their way after confusing our generals with convenient disinformation. I know that our Prime Minister, had gone to China where was given a special gift by the Chinese President, Chow-en-Lei. I see it now as a day light bluff that worked, for we started regarding the Chinese as friends and brothers, as 'bhai, bhai'.

No one expected China in our midst, and I know

we have no money to spend, though gold could yet save the country. Nehru requested donations of gold to be converted into bonds for future redemption. Considering me as a pillar of the community, I'm chosen for the job, even supplied with a little weighing scale to keep records. May my mathematics be equal to the task. It's a matter of amazement how even the poorest respond to the call. A poor village woman brings a tiny nose pin that she has kept for her daughter's dowry. She has done it for Punditji.

As our first Prime Minster after Independence, Nehru was building a nation but it was the border war that hurried his death.

'You know nothing about gold, Prami. How stupid of these people to trust you.'

Bill pronounces this judgment from the heights of the Nalda club, a buttered rum in his hand. The club-house had soon became his principality, the glass of rum, his sceptre.

Futile to explain, yet I have a go.

'Our army is in trouble; we've been caught off-guard. Our Air Force can't fly at those fourteen thousand-foot heights. We're short of rations, winter clothing, heavy weapons, roads to the front line and, there's even no money to pay our foot soldiers, *jawans*.'

'Poor planning from you Indians.' High and mighty, hoity-toity, Bill plays deaf ear to my concerns. How dare he debase my hero! This man must be celebrated and not be used as a tool to exercise Bill's wit. He has fought a passionate, non-violent battle I must celebrate this remarkable man. He has remained my hero right from the days when I picked up his story from a book I borrowed from the Colonel's library.

> *Nehru passed away soon after in 1964, leaving a note.*
> *'The woods are lovely dark and deep*
> *But I have promises to keep*
> *And miles and miles to go before I sleep.'*
> Robert Frost: *Stopping by Woods on a Snowy Evening*

I too have a promise to keep, a payback for Bill's behaviour, but I shall bide my time till the right moment comes. I must have been a feeble woman to be pulled down so easily. This supposed holiday has become a farce and I blame Father for extending it.

The lotus may have bloomed at the beginning, but now I saw the fearful growth rooting in wonderland. We must get out of here, one way or another. The remedy came from a bear; my cue as well.

> *'Exit, pursued by a bear.'*
> Shakespeare: *The Winter's Tale* (stage directions)

The Saga of the Bill
and the Bear

Father has to make frequent trips to the mines. On this God-given occasion, he had asked Bill to accompany two Japanese buyers for their on-the-spot survey of our operation. As they are doing their stuff, making notes, an excited villager gushes in, out of breath, announcing, gesticulating that a bear has been spotted just above them in a cave.

Bears are deep alcoholic somnambulists when crashed out after a binge on mahua berries when in season' it's so easy to step on them without noticing. Our guide lifted his singlet, revealing deep claw marks from neck to navel.

I've made so many sorties into forests, but never run into bears; they generally hide deep in the rocks, normally asleep during daytime sporting a V on their chest. V, for what? Victory over intruders, probably, they trespass on his territory.

To find a sloth bear so close to a busy mine appears to be a heaven-sent opportunity. So, off they go, scrambling through thorny bushes and rocks till they reach a gap in a roundish, grey rock.

Bill, the great white hunter, has handed over the Father's rifle to the driver walking alongside. Unarmed, my hero takes charge, and goes boldly into the cave, all macho. It's nothing short of a spaghetti western.

'Nothing here,' he hollers.

As if on cue a growl fills the cave, and before you can say 'Jack Robinson', or whatever they say in Japanese, a shaggy black bear rolls out from the cave with Bill.

It's a steep slope, the impetus of the collision makes both lose balance, and they roll down the hill, Bill's buttocks firmly locked into the bear's jaws. The driver points the gun but the tumbling pair makes an impossible target, sometimes he sees a part of Bill, sometimes the white V on the bear's chest. The Japanese stand electrified, no one raises the camera. Eventually, Bill manages to free an arm and punches the bear on the nose. With a deep-throated growl, the animal vanishes; the driver fires a shot and Japs fire many more with their cameras, but all they get is the departing rear.

A defeated army bring a bleeding Bill home to me. Looking at his condition, I can't but help feeling sorry for him. The canines had dug deep into the flesh, I can see blood oozing from the holes made by the bear's teeth; a helpless mand trying to be brave.

I lie Bill down on his chest and start to clean his wounds and all I've got is an old-fashioned razor. He's a hairy old bugger, this husband of mine. Bill squiggles, and bucks, and growls, but I soldier on. The company doctor gives Bill the first injection but the full treatment needs twenty-two, all to be inserted into the abdomen. It's a gruesome procedure; the brain of a rabid sheep is processed, and a serum created for the victim. Doesn't bear thinking about. To add to it, Bill doesn't need locals surrounding him. He complains that all they do is salaam, some even grin. I see his depression creeping in. He has had enough of the third world.

To get better he needs social chitter-chatter, something akin to a pint in a pub. For that there's the Jesuit from the school waiting in the wings. I can offer Bill an educated God man at his disposal and give myself a little boost.

He now makes it a habit to stay overnight for rollicking evenings of sacramental wine, drained down with bollocking songs. In the end Bill gets his company and the Jesuit gets Bill's booze. Call it compromise.

I was getting along famously with this arrangement till Father recalls us. Better doctors in Calcutta.

1965-1968

Calcutta:
Three years at Tivoli Court

> *'We are sailing down the Hooghly River, inland towards
> Calcutta. I am a younger man, and I travel with a
> group of Polish Jewish refugees. Our lives are cheap
> and our pockets are empty.'*
> Bem Le Hunte: *Where the Pepper Grows*

When we returned from Barbil I had hoped we would soon return to England but the moment we got off the train, Mother Bear was waiting, ready to pounce and gather the excited children into the imported yellow Buick. Hurrah for the outing! Father was welcoming, as well but seemed concerned about Bill's recovery; he had arranged for a consultant from the Tropical School of Medicine. In fact, he had arranged everything beforehand. we had walked into a trap. I'm slipping away from this blind hero worship of my adored parent. I can see his mind in action.

He knew perfectly well that the injections would soon finish, yet he was still not prepared to let the falcon escape. Rumours had reached him from Barbil that Bill was slacking off. He never reported back to head office; instead, missives arrived on his activities at the Nalda club.

The wily falconer had an answer; the falcon would be kept in his mews. Bill must remain in Calcutta. He found us a place to live as he did in Cambridge, but this time it was an impressive colonial property ready and waiting for Bill to fantasise about living a grand life What's more, it was near his house.

We are settled in a converted mansion, near his home. The proximity speaks for itself. Our living room is a huge back verandah lined with lofty columns painted in black and white stripes giving it a Franco colonial ambience. Perhaps, Father must have envisaged that with a name like Le Hunte, Bill would fit well with a colonial back drop. At least his friends at his club could be glanced away from the truth that Bill's father was a mere a bank clerk.

He had top-and-tailed his son-in-law, making him appear squeaky clean, ready to be displayed as an officer of his firm.

In addition, Calcutta life has to be made more lotus friendly. Tivoli Park is a service apartment with a western cook at our disposal, own car, own chauffer and Bill's own Man Friday and obviously membership of the Victoria club. But the nub of it all was that Bill was forced to work with Father, and it didn't pan out at all for either of them.

Father's ashtray is piled high with a mountain of cigarette butts. He chain-smokes when he's stressed.

It's clear that Bill has had enough of Father. He had started in England by calling him, 'A good bloke', but now, it's more of, 'Your bloody father'. Things are wrong between them. Bill is expected to put in proper work, take on responsibility for his growing family. The lotus-eater indulgence has gone. As a result, Bill comes home irritated and takes it out on me when it really should be with Mother who hangs around strategically at mealtimes. When he tries to horse around with the twins, putting each on his lap hand-picking little okra pieces to put into their mouths, she changes the menu. Bill gets uptight and votes with his feet; he walks out. He is out manoeuvred by this lady. He's had more than enough of my mother, I don't blame him. Touché!

The tinder from the bear bite had lit a little spark but I allowed it to get extinguished unnoticed amidst the battleground of home. So much awaits me in Calcutta the second time round. Not only did I get a parttime job as an English lecturer at Loreto college but I have also become the Calcutta correspondent of *Femina*, the prime magazine for women. What an entrée into high society whose parties and high jinks I had to report. How low can a blue stocking sink? However much the rise be juicy, revenge is sweeter: Bill is permitted to accompany me as an 'extra'. Nobody takes any note of him. I'm getting my revenge for the years he put me down. Totally relishing my new lifestyle, I was becoming another Shylock, savouring my pound of flesh. With all my supposed knowledge of Shakespeare, I had forgotten that Justice was blind. Her scales tipped against me.

Was it my self-induced blindness that allowed him to escape? I go burning candle after candle and had overlooked that the worm had turned.

Bill joins the Rowing Club of Calcutta that *ipso-facto* is only for whites. Not that they openly eschew segregation, but there is no Indian membership; it's a dangerous inner circle. Eight pair of eyes stare unblinking as I turn up.

'Look, the wife again. On your bike, mate.'

Bollocks to you, gentlemen of the boat. Yet, they are right. I must pack up my bags and his bollocks in my old kit bag; it's time to get us out of Calcutta, in fact, to leave India.

Fools in anger rush in where angels fear to tread. What about the consequences? My mother is getting old and I have a duty as their only child to make amends and be beside them through their last years.

As for Mother, what can you do with a rebel. A fifth column in their midst? Although I resented every effort Mother made to control my children, they are a happy captive bunch munching crisps and downing Campa Cola. Eventually, her ministrations, slip easily down my throat, as well, no crunch, no punch, just soggy, marshmallow love.

I'm at the cross roads yet again, the pull of my home land is still strong so, remain. I'm cushioned in my own country and there are choppy waters at the other end. Just having a Cambridge degree won't float. The demography of the nation is changing. Ironically, with input of immigration from Europe and the developing countries, Britain is becoming less global! Take a lesson from the blue eyes at the Rowing Club. You will be going to a racist country. You will need more power to your elbow to survive. Remember the message of Huck Finn; sometimes you will get hurt, but you'll survive. Make an effort to restore your marriage. After almost decade you must know the man well. Try to remember what pumps the man.

I know that Bill enjoys company, a merry-mix of laughter and booze. Was it not so in Bombay on the ship's deck? Was it not the reason I introduced the Jesuit at his bedside? Provide him the medicine he needs. Re aligning myself, I realise that I have responded too harshly to Bill's Rowing club for he's never been a sporty man. If he needs to stretch his limbs, right through the middle of Calcutta, flows the mighty Hooghly and beyond lies the Barrackpore Yacht club that could prove more enticing than the Rowing club. We can get our own little dinghy and the children can join us too. It also has an international membership; I want Bill to feel in control once again. Far too long he's been playing second fiddle to Father and me. We become members of the club and make weekend sorties from the city.

Hooghly is really a part of the holy Ganges as she makes her way to the Bay of Bengal. All fishermen know her habits; at certain times of the year, a tidal bore charges through the water thundering its way upstream. Riding the bore is a challenge for the daring, more like standing on the top of Everest. and for Bill, it will be more invigorating than fighting a bear.

Imagine the Le Hunte family about twenty miles upstream. We now have a fourteen-foot dinghy called Karl O'Laf, that we bought from a homeward bound German couple. When we picnic in the club grounds and the bar waiter fills the plate with crisps, Bill falls to them like an out-of-control child. He frequently gets my sometime smile.

Arjun, particularly takes a shine to the boat and, when we're not competing, Bill takes him for a little sail. He loves calling out, 'Ready about, heave-ho!' to his captain, commanding him to turn the boat round. Great sight to see, family in action; that's the way I like things to be. Throughout our time in Barbil we've all lead separate lives.

Throwing caution to the winds, I want to heave-ho with my husband. It's important for us to do things together, to light a spark left by the bear. Tending to Bill's buttocks has got me closer to him; time to slap them into action!

Bill was quick on the uptake, especially with viable admirers watching from the shore. As we set off a club member, turning his eyes to the heavens, tries to calm our nerves, 'The Force be with you,' he calls out. But the Force had better things to do. Like a roaring wall of water, the bore strikes! Karl O'Laf bucks and rears, but Bill holds on to the tiller, keeping the boat at exactly ninety degrees to the oncoming bore. We've been warned that even the slightest tilt could capsize the boat. What a sense of triumph as we ride atop and the water passes on, but it seems to be dragging a memento.

The power of the impact has released a wooden paddle from its catch. I lean sideways to retrieve it, and off I go overboard doing the opposite of what I've been warned.

Pushed upstream by the tide, my bobbing head is still visible above my life jacket. Roll after roll, the water splashes over me; I can feel the violence of the thrust… till it gets slower and slower until I'm stopped against a boulder by the river side.

How far have I drifted? I can only see palm trees bent with the wind. No Bill in sight; he's probably steered the boat to safety.

I must have passed out till I hear the chug-chug of an outboard motor. The rescue boat has arrived with two men on board. On arrival at the club's jetty, a dripping scare crow steps out.

Arjun stands rigid with tension, the twins hardly recognise me and Bem has three fingers in her mouth, but where's Bill?

I can him muttering from afar.

'You stupid woman!'

No interest, no compassion; he's packing the boot of the car. It is he who has made the decision.

One knows when the battle is lost. It was Custer's last stand.

1968-83

Getting stuck in Richmond

As soon as we returned from India, Bill 'abandoned' me for the swinging sixties. The lotus garb was wearing thin and the lads at the rowing club had fed him stories of the buzz of a new era. Obviously, that left me waltzing ungainly to the buzz of the hoover.

I made my bed from old sheets in the charity shop and now I must lie on the sheets of others.

Bill found himself a job as a trainee with IBM. Miraculously, with the little money he had saved from his salary, he foraged in select localities and found a neglected house in Richmond regarded as one of the posh areas around London. All very well, but what about me? What a comedown from the grandiose living to find oneself on the wrong side of a railway track! I'm used to thundering from below from the Mosaboni mines, but now it's all around.

Commuter trains to London stampede by our wooden garage. It's the kind of place and estate agent might market as having plenty of potential, but requires total renovation' It had sailed seven seas with its captain who regarded the place as his ship and rang seven bells to summon the crew.

It played hell with the neighbours. When we arrived, they were delighted to see the back of him, but Bill had no problem with its condition of Sheen Park. It's the locality that matters and the Tudors had put their stamp on Richmond Green. I had not the slightest idea of his snobbery; he must have acquired it from uncle Len. He was happy to ignore the rubbish within. It boasted a lounge with a worn-out brownish damp carpet and an old piano with missing keys, looking quite like a dentist's half-finished job. Home is where the heart is, Bill's heart has blown elsewhere.

Mini-skirted girls exposed knickers as they sat across from him in the Tube. What breakfast delight, what movement in his pants! Mary Quant had declared that fashion had shifted from 'tit to cunt'; that certainly made Bill wag his tail. But what 'goes up' in the morning goes limp, comes down when he returns home, for home is burnt toast for tea. I know nothing about running a home and the Baby Belling isn't not equal to the job but it makes for good business for fish fingers and broken eggs from South Africa! I'm fed up with compulsory domesticity.

Unfortunately, my qualification from St. Bede's is not recognised here and I'm forced to enrol for an Advanced Diploma in psychology and sociology at the Institute of Education in London. I have phoned Father in Calcutta and we agreed that he will pay for the course till I get myself a proper job.

Bill is quite happy with the arrangement; it costs him nothing and his occasional homelife can carry on as normal for I've already made sure that imported broken eggs make the quickest omelette.

With an absentee husband I tried to amuse myself by joining a class for adults on creative writing. It's Prami, thinly disguised, laughing at herself rather than her condition. Take one look at her story:

> *It's an historical imperative that everything must change with the times. Even a mere Christmas tree must bend with this ruling, and don the style of the day. The tree bore the signature of my shopping, and more so reflected on my weak character; a mother who easily gave in to the pester power of her demanding brats. An ignorant woman to boot! Whole shelves from Woolworths were driven by the prevailing winds to scatter themselves on the tree. A Christmas tree was meant to be eaten! And, if the shopping records told the truth, consumed as cheaply as possible, none of your Swiss delicacies filled with of Lindt and mint bars dared compete.*

Not a sign of whinging here for there will be many more Christmases to come. As in Calcutta, I'm determined to taste British life to the full.

Surely the best time to dig into another slice of cake and sweeten my resolve. It tastes sweeter now, more Christmassy.

St. Bede's calls. There is a well-known dramatic society in Twickenham. If I join, I can be Sir Anthony Absolute once again or an Antonia Absolute, the key word being 'absolute,' absolutely free of Bill. I run the idea past Bill. He has never been a fanatic of the peanut play but this idea amuses him.

Bill quips, 'If you wish to do something to occupy yourself, best you prance on the stage.'

'Why not?' I say and keep him to his word.

'But do try to come back a little earlier from now on for the children will be alone.'

'Bully for them,' he mumbles. An evening with his après work buddies makes him a mirror image of the man at the bottle party.

The children have heard this and take it as licence to riot. With credentials from St Bede's, I was admitted at director level to The Richmond Shakespeare Society, where I first produced my one-act play called *'The Sandbox'* by Edward Albee. I was drawn to a protagonist in her second childhood. She was contained in a sandbox on the beach; she is an opinionated, garrulous old bird. No need for three guesses for my choice; it was the lady with the frown. I'm blowing away the cobwebs of the past.

*

It's September, 1968. Time for school. The girls are admitted to schools on the slopes of the prestigious Richmond Hill. Bill has tried to calm my apprehension about the colour prejudice they might well encounter.

'They'll be just fine,' was his fatuous reply. 'We live in a middle-class suburb. No trash in our midst' It's the year of Enoch Powell's infamous 'rivers of blood' speech, warning the country against the flux of immigrants.

*'Like the Roman, I seem to see the river Tiber foaming
with much blood,'*

It becomes an inglorious autumn for the twins, for despite their school being in an elitist area, they receive the sting of caustic, racial remarks about being dirty. Bill has admitted Arjun to a private prep school where the boys are more akin to the children of ex-pats of the tennis courts in Mosaboni. He was hoping to give his only son a flying start. It was the wrong choice to bring about class distinction within the same family. Although Arjun fitted well in his environment the twins are embarrassed by their mother taking them to school in a sari.

'Paky', the pupils call them, but to me, they look Caucasian. Could it be their names, Anjali and Ashika sound strange to their limited English ears? Or was the bullying because their English is poor. Mother out of policy spoke to them only in Hindi; Buddi ayah knew only a few words of the land of the *sahibs*, and Bill and I contributing with English whenever we spoke to them, were unable tip the scale. Whatever may be the case, their profile, in the eyes of their peers felt foreign.

On arrival the twins had asked me, 'Whatever made you bring us here; we were so much better off with Nani in Calcutta?' It was impossible to explain to them in these tender years that both their mother and father were at the crossroads of their life, and had to make choices, and some choices can be hard, and returning 'home' was done in good faith.

Busy with picking holes in English children, it is now I who has to face the ugly truth rearing its head. I don't want my children playing with a neighbour who happens to be a plumber's daughter. In India plumbing is considered a low caste profession and it's *infra dig* to allow my children to mix with these people. I look in the mirror darkly and say to myself, I have come to settle in England and carried all my filthy prejudices with me.

'Off with their heads!' demanded the Queen of Hearts.

'Off with my sari!' say I, and anon appear the airy thighs through which the British wind blows.

With my new mini-skirt, I'm now fully prepared for an English school replete with children out of control. It's a bear garden where I first got temporary employment as a supply teacher. In the seventies it was designated as an ESN school, meaning it was meant for those whom borough recognises as being educationally subnormal.

To put it bluntly, they hosted black children of the Windrush generation alongside those with special needs. innocent youngsters get branded for life.

From the nadir to the pinnacle, I ring many more bells, and keep on rising till I find myself as Head of English in England's most prestigious girls' school where to my astonishment, in 1988, I get a phone call from The Secretary of State for Education to join the Kingman Committee that he had set up set up to create a profile English language to be used in all schools. Of all the English teachers in the country, only two were selected to be flag-bearers of our subject, and it was yours truly who was given the voice. And didn't I use it! I want the teaching of English to diverse communities to be a level playing field. Windrush, you are on board.

Camping and Pranking

Progressing through English schools was a cake walk for me, but for my children it could be hard grind. What helped them survive were the holidays when Bill shed his office garb and took us camping, albeit on a slender budget. It was the simplicity and spontaneity of our joy that defined the litmus. We may not have the latest equipment, but our trusty old friend, the Ford Popular, is by our side. Like a knight is armed for a battle our white car is ceremoniously prepared for battle adventure. We'd gone to the camping shop on Richmond High Street, and bought ourselves the cheapest orange tent with a pennant. It's just large enough to hold all six of us on the floor. Five people can sleep in a line, and there's even a little space left sideways for a tiny camp bed for the complaining mother! Everything like cooking pots, camping stove, mugs and spoons, etc. remain in the car. How dare they fight for space with the somnambulant sardines?

For the children it was great fun setting up the framework of the tent, pulling down the canvas and staking the guy ropes into the ground. We now have a five-star residence and ready to be served. 'Waiter, bring out the chips.' We seem to be in Barrackpore yacht club once more.

Bill appears to be an experienced camper right from the start. We always camped quite near a stream where we could get water to clean ourselves and the dishes, both with a questionable finish. Once we camped by a loch where a cheeky salmon is splashing pure silver, jumping high, enticing us to catch it. We've got a fishing rod. All of us take our turns at the salmon, who is surely an expert at the game, notoriously canny, jumping up to tempt and nosing down in a flash to appear elsewhere in the loch.

As for camping spots the children have begun to think they are experts in finding the right spots to put down the tent, but they never agree, while I wait impatiently by the car, being attacked by an army of midges. I've had enough of mosquitoes in India. Why the hell have they come to Scotland?

Answer: because it's always so late when we arrive; there are far too many pubs along the way, shelves filled with tempting bottles of single malt, and for me other distractions, tourist paraphernalia and renegade book stores. The peat bogs around squelch with history of clans warring, ghosts lurking!

> *'The Deil had business on his hand.'*
> Robert Burns: *Tam O'Shanter*

We are in a land of magic, far away from urban Richmond. Bill and the children love long walks through the moors, and as with the Pied Piper, they race behind. Sometimes, he holds out his fingers and they hang on to each one, stumbling along over purple heather. Holidays cannot be fun without their father within touching distance.

We even took a continental camping holiday all the way to Spain and I have clear memories of us jollying on the beach when Bill pulls out a small child from the water, picks her up as in play and with gay abandon, tosses her straight into the waves. Out comes a screaming child, but it's not Bem! He ate humble paella of course.

As a finale we drop in at a beer fest in Germany, enjoying the bumping, thumping, drinking songs of the time. I enjoy such chaos to the hilt, the thespian in me coming out as I sway with the tourists.

> *Trink, trink, Brüderlein trink*
> *Laß doch die Sorgen zu Haus.*

Over and over again we are still in the same Ford Popular and squashed up in the same little tent. Who cares? I'm happy to have Bill beside me at last.

The children are unanimous in giving the thumbs up to such riotous holidays; they still remember them with nostalgia, and wish those three years hadn't ended so abruptly when Bill found himself a love nest.

My grown children

While camping days were super fun, teen-age was a nightmare. I remember my own. Would history repeat itself?

Money can't buy you love, sing the Beatles. But you can buy it if you wear hot pants! But who wears the pants? The latest fashion of itsy-bitsy 'knickers' creates a no-holes-barred confrontation between the twins and me. I find it excessive; the girls think me regressive. Sheen Park becomes a theatre of war. The twins take up stations, 'defiance vs compliance', and look out for allies. Bill immediately joins the troops; he stops himself being called Daddy, and enrols as a fellow-fighter, 'William'. Now, he's their buddy, and their old female foe, that's me, goes down the ranks as 'Fatty'. I would be insulted if I didn't see the funny side. I will be a laughing figure in a large uniform.

However, I'm still the captain of the ship and will not be boarded by pirates. It was the birth of Genghis Khan with the commanding voice of a dictator. Did I do anything wrong? Yes, I bust the family.

Ashi flees the ship; Anju retires to the attic with our little dog, Flash for comfort; Bem gets lost amongst her liberal friends she has collected away from the house and Arjun loses contact with the home-front now, that he is a university student.

Have I become an empty-nester? I wouldn't look at it that way. I' not the kind of woman who wants her child hanging on to her sari. This teen age thing is a little blimp that will go away.

With hindsight, I made a mistake of dressing twins in identical clothes. Now they have every right to express themselves their own way.

Anju slips into loose skirts, hangs her hair long with dingle-dangle jewellery, the hippy fashion of the day. She flower-powered her way through the university of Leeds and eventually qualifies as a teacher. Her flat is an exciting wooden 'O'. With every act the space changes: What was a bedroom shapes up as a kitchen, and should the plot require, the kitchen squeezes itself into the hall and its work top thrives as her study. Even her bathroom does a walkabout into the coal shed and the giant doll house takes over the garden. This is not the woman who lives in a shoe; she lodges in a revolving roundabout. I regard her as a better theatre director than me; she has talented cast of four of her own little people whom she adores.

Ashi's image is more professional, you won't catch her in jeans. Quick-witted, she can seize the moment. At the age of eighteen in 1979, she vanishes one evening to her grandmother's house that is empty because Doll is in hospital where she eventually dies, and leaves Ashi behind as the official squatter who can invite anyone she chooses. She has run away from home because of Fatty, and William supports her even though I beg of him to bring her home. Net result, she does poorly in exams but ups herself and qualifies later in business studies. She has found her métier. She's a money-conscious lass who checks her bank statement the first thing in the morning. There are no flies on Ashi; they have run away off to Australia where she lives now.

I was not able to meet her for years. They tell me time was hard, and unrelenting. How long can one allow life to slip by doing the dishes? But she made a fist of it and ended up with her own bijoux cottage near Twickenham Green. Bully for her and her spirit of enterprise.

Penny makes pounds, cents rise up as dollars. Her motto: The universe provides She will eventually become a southern hemisphere entrepreneur, hopping around like a kangaroo through Australia, to run away from the heat of the sun. Unusual, for that's what the English seek when they go down under, but then she's neither a mad dog or an English woman. She is simply Ashi. Let the universe provide for one who deserves.

Bem, a newcomer to the teens is not overtly rebellious yet she rehouses herself on Richmond Green with a group of young people miles apart from middleclass Richmond. They spend quality time attending courts where their friends are being evicted from 'squatting' in empty Hammersmith flats. I suppose it could be called the emancipated sixties. She now has a pied-à-terre in a tree house to keep the night walkabout possums at bay. She's a wonder; she has elephants with headlights, her pepper comes from far away and she gets seduced by silence. I'm not being funny, nor attempting the Times cross word. These are clues coming from Bem herself. She's a novelist of acclaim who delves into her roots in India. *Jai Hind* to you.

Arjun flees to Brunel University where he makes his den, touching base only *kabhi kahbhi*, that's once in a while as the occasion demands or girlfriends allow. My word, isn't he growing up! I've bought him a signet ring with the Le Hunte coat of arms. It was uncle Len who impressed him with their family's genealogy. He traced the Le Huntes right back to Henry II when the Norman Le Venere, the hunter, was anglicised to its present form.

I am still known among the oldies in Pembrokeshire as Mrs Le Hunté. Feels very noble. Arjun is a *burra sahib* in word and deed. He lives in a detached house near Kew

Gardens, his bar is stocked with the choicest French wine, and I see him as an equerry of Bill for the the relationship established from day one over the bathtub! Each child is very special and unique.

With such a posh name on offer, why did Bill not barter for a better job? It would look good on a letter-head or a flourish after a signature. But he has dragged on with I.B.M. happy with the present of pints and pub. It can only be his downfall. He once told me that during an interview for promotion. His bosses got the impression that all he was thinking was his next cup of coffee! Some people are born great, some disappear into the espresso.

As for Prami, she took to the streets but not in the way you think.

A greenhorn politician

Behold Prami! Not on any road to Everest, I find myself in an urban jungle. I'm standing bold as brass on the high street, my assets on display. Not my bum, not her bust, but my brain. I must think out of the box. The domestic thing has gone wrong. The Captain of Dramatics has not been cast as a homemaker, rather as a performer. Why not make use of the skills on offer? When I look at myself as a child, a little poetaster emerges sipping tea and making drawing room conversation making drawing room conversion as in a Noël Coward play, with a skipping rope for background music.

Having grossly mismanaged domestic warfare, I need another platform to sharpen my skills so why not politics where many fakes are given a role to play. Like a knight on a chessboard, I make a hopscotch move to the Hight street and masquerade as the shadow councillor for my ward. I know there is no such position as shadow opposition, but many are familiar with shadow positions in parliament and people will believe if you bleat long enough.

I have leapfrogged into the committee of my ward and risen to pole position through my zeal for supporting Thatcher.

> *'It may be the cock that crows,*
> *but it is the hen that lays the eggs.'*
> Margaret Thatcher

I take my stand in the high street with my blue rosette and further the Conservatives in loquacious opposition. I engage pedestrian traffic on issues of concern. Richmond has a Liberal Council that is planning major cuts to local amenities.

'Friends, don't we all have a right to protest?' I argue with conviction. Shakespeare's Mark Antony comes in handy with his rhetorical flourishes. I distribute my leaflets to shoppers and push some through the front doors; useful stuff to read over a cuppa.

My leaflet is different; it's in the form of a ballad, a call to arms from an elderly park bench about to be culled to make room for new development by the Council. The Park is the mainstay for local communities; her voice will be heard with the next election coming in May. The leaflet cries out for action for 'old timbers remember a lot'.

> 'When motor bike recruits in their steel tipped boots
> Volley and thunder my ground
> There is deadly danger around.
> The pub shuts its doors; a vagrant snore
> Beneath sheets of newspaper dies he …
> No policemen around. …

> Till the body was found.
> Poor Tom. I knew him well.
> He was a war hero.
> He defended a bridge
> Near Two Sister's Ridge
> When the Falkland battle was on.
> Not a verse nor a prayer was read by the mayor
> But a photo-op didn't take long!
> I'll show you the guile
> Behind his political smile.
> Record every word that he said.
> 'We've said with one voice
> We don't have a choice
> This dirty little bench must go!
> She'll rally the crowd who'll cry out aloud
> That it has to be Council that goes!

All my frustration at home come out in my fury. To add to it, I'm honing my skills as a writer. My body feels a release such I'd never known before.

But it came at a cost; my health gave way. I was no longer a spring chicken, my body squawked: two sessions at Northwick Park hospital on matters of the heart and a rampant pulse on matters of the man. What began as jockeying for position in Barbil has now turned into an open war.

Father who has come to visit us took in the situation at a glance. While we all sat at the table one lunchtime, I mention that was I feeling a little rough and needed to go upstairs and rest. Giving me just a little time to drift off, Bill galvanises his troops.

'Let's go upstairs and wake up Fatty.' The children jump up in a flash, but Father just as quick, unceremoniously pushes them down, thundering,

'This is *no way* to behave towards your mother!'

Mother told me later, in confidence, that he was so furious at Bill that he came very near to landing him a blow. Yes, the previous antagonists have now bonded. The lion lies down with the lamb.

Later Father came to me in the bedroom and careful of every word, he gave me a warning.

'Prami, we have brought up the Indian way; we believe your children have a duty to respect you. But from what I see, things are very wrong. Just look at your health! You are pulled down. I'm getting older and weaker, and will not be around to help you, but listen clearly to my words. Your children's values are very British.' He stumbles on his words. 'Watch out! It's my duty to warn you. Thinking you are weak, make sure they don't go for your money and treat you kindly.'

I'm lost for words. Never before had he spoken so intimately. The old man can barely walk, yet he stumbled up the stairs to sit beside me and tell me the truth, however stark it may seem.

Four months later, Father died.

1979

Delhi: My Father Dies

> *'My father didn't tell me how to live; he lived, and let me watch him do it.'*
> Clarence Beddington Kelland

It's New Year's Eve, a policeman knocks on the door with the news that my beloved Father has passed away. His last words echo back. Although they were made up as warning, what came through felt like overflowing love. He was my backbone, my source of strength.

Father was only seventy, but he has already had two heart attacks. I flew from Richmond to see him in hospital the first time. He was covered in machines and plastic bags, but he still insists on reminding his consultant,

'You have to allow me to move around, doctor. All my life, I have been a man of the field.'

I sat helplessly beside him, wishing I was his son able to follow this great man of the field. The red-earth wilderness, the mines he had discovered, were his life. And his only daughter was his life as well. Like the timber he sold to the mines, he was my support for all those years and I took his presence for granted. Never to be judgemental of the wild girl in his house, recognising that in many ways I was like him.

After the policeman came to the door, I pull my son out of university and both of us take a plane to Delhi, for I require Arjun to perform the last rites. It will be long journey on the plane and

I fill up time by getting Arjun to understand the life story of this greatest of men.

Father's birthplace holds an Arabian Nights fascination for me. You might know of Kipling country, with The Khyber Pass connecting India to Afghanistan, a desolate, raw, unconquered place. Yes, Arjun has read *Kim*.

'All the British power failed to control the insurgent, underbelly population, and neither can Pakistan now. But farther south is the Bolan Pass for camel caravans arriving to trade. The entry point is Kulachi, your grandfather's father's village. It flourishes as an exchange post. The caravans empty their ware to be dispersed throughout India and Ceylon, and take back silk and spices to the West.'

'Is that why they sell Ceylon tea in supermarkets?' Arjun has connected.

'Probably the result of early trade,' I improvise.

'They seem very backward over there using camels and stuff.'

'The terrain wouldn't allow your bicycle. It's all open desert.' I'm a little annoyed at his insensitivity.

'Where did they shit?' he continues. It seems an important question to this young Westerner. I couldn't resist a riposte.

'People or camels?'

'People of course.'

I had asked this very question to my grandmother. The toilet on the roof was an open hole, with an open door; she sent her daughters up in pairs to do their business, so one of them can hold up a sheet over the open door.

'They shat down a hole as we did when camping.'

Ah! those were the long-ago days. I turn to Arjun to remind him of happier times but he's fallen asleep.

From such a humble beginning to end up in Bristol to study civil engineering must have been a giant leap for a frontier man.

When we arrive at the home that he built in Delhi, both sides of my family are already assembled. If sorrow has a face, look at his youngest brother; if anyone is needed to hug Mother, Kamla Masi is right beside. All are dressed in white, the garb of mourning. Joss sticks burn incense and when I touch I him, Father's hand is cold and hard as marble with veins coming up in variegated lines.

He has been placed on ice blocks on the floor, for in his hometown, the dying are sent to their Maker with humility.

It's the normal custom in India to cremate on the day of the death, but permission for delay has been taken on account of Arjun and I being abroad.

The hearse is waiting, and within half an hour we move to the cremation ground where my uncle has got a wood pyre assembled with a priest beside him in white dhoti with a *tilak* on his forehead like Shyama. Father is placed on the pyre; Arjun is supported tenderly as he struggles to bring the burning stick of fire to his nana, and then the sacred Hindu rites can begin.

It will take two days for the ashes to cool. Arjun will have to go to collect his grandfather's ashes and bones. With loving grace, we call them his 'flowers' and take them to Hardwar where they will be immersed in the holy Ganges. It will be a gruesome task for a boy with the sensibilities of the West. But for me there is no fear; death is awesome reality. of death.

In my childhood I have been forced to come face to face with bloodless, lifeless bodies. The road outside our house in Calcutta is the highway of the dead. A corpse is being carried on a bamboo pallet on the shoulders of four men. The body of the man is covered with white swaddling, but the face is always exposed, the mask of death. I could hear the chant anywhere in our house.

> *'Bol Hari, Hari Bol, Bol Hari,'*
> 'Take the name of God, and take it again.'

I startle, freeze, and drawn as by a magnet of fear, I make for the window and look out: child face staring at dead face, a moment of desperate union. It's happening now as I stare at Father's face. With such a bond of love, we can never part.

Richmond: The Captain of Dramatics revisited

Arriving back from the trauma of Father's cremation I need time to settle myself, come to terms with my grief. After the warmth and love poured on us in India, this country comes across as soul-free. I have come home after losing a father and have not the slightest interest in the weather. Is it necessary to chirrup away on the perquisites of summer? Yes, it's a lovely day and the cuckoo has done her stuff. Why is it so difficult for people to share my grief? Even a silent moment of togetherness will do or a slow-motion hug, I'm unsettled and especially and irritated, with Bill who has given the topic a wide berth. I must not brood if I mean to move on and breathe some fresh air.

The Thames is agog with pleasure boats, bikinis and the Barmy Army. I'm sitting on a bench, nibbling my cake. It's a warm day and the pub is in full throat. The Barmy Arms is next to our theatre and odours come through of a kitchen at work. I tap away to their songs with a glass of Old Peculiar in my hand. Don't forget, I'm a cricket fanatic myself. I know the ins and outs of this place. Once, I sweated there myself. I was planning ahead on what to do should Bill leave me which could be on the cards. I applied to Watney's for training on managing a pub.

It would be so much more fun chatting with the regulars, than toiling away in our kitchen. I had enjoyed the impromptu chats while campaigning. I enjoy a good gossip and can generate a giggle. That's a skill in itself.

> *Potato was deep in the dark underground,*
> *Tomato, above in the light.*
> *The little Tomato was ruddy and round,*
> *The little Potato was white.*
> *And redder and redder she rounded above,*
> *And paler and paler he grew,*
> *And neither suspected a mutual love*
> *Till they met in a Brunswick stew*
> John B. Tabb: *The Tryst*

Now the stew is overcooked, in fact a glutinous mess. I'm no longer on any road to Everest. I'm in a sludge. Whither hence?

I look around; the notice by the bank marks the time of high tide, for Thames, like Hooghly, is a tidal river and people have been caught out by rising water. It has happened to me during a rehearsal of Marlowe's *Tamburlaine* where the pomp and circumstance within the play made time disappear as armies marched to a backdrop of skulls and marshal music from Wagner, and the beauty a woman's face launched a thousand ships.

Well, the waters rose and the mouldy car seat stank for a fortnight. Not to worry, it's all bearable when you win an award for the most original production of the year. Probably, that's where my skills really lie, my quirky imagination.

Why be moody today? Celebrate your achievement; take another bite of your cake. I cast my eyes at the notice board, I have less than half an hour left before high tide. In haste I collect my belongings.

I have been asked to direct *Much Ado about Nothing* by Shakespeare. The summer show is always held in the open-air. The play opens with the lads returning home after a war. so why not mark the event; let loose a flight of doves into the sky? All very well, but for warlock's sake, I'm no wizard; I have no chant to entice doves to my pecking table. The imagination goes on over drive as I munch my cake; a crumb drops from my hand and hey presto, all around me gathered the pigeons!

Yes, pigeons will have to do. As it happens, there's a pigeon fancier's club not so far away. I approach their good will, promising free tickets for their trouble. As *Much Ado about Nothing* happens to be an evening production, the opening scene tallies with the sunset when trained pigeons, once let out, will find their way home. Fortunately, on the opening night it's a clear evening. As soon their baskets open, the birds set off with the sound of rapid flutter; they circle over their audience in the setting sun, then gather together in formation as in an air show and wing their way home, donating splats to the clapping audience. Would that Bill be there to receive a blessing! The very thought of it clears my depression.

Let there be many more Prami-style plays to follow. Fatty has come into her own. Break a leg or better still knock down a pint.

It's 1977, the Queen's Silver Jubilee, the nation celebrates, so do I. Extraordinary turnaround for the little freedom fighter who longed to see the backside of the British empire.

I start Christmas wassails all over local pubs. Not all that different from shenanigans at Moulin Rouge except the largesse was not pounds but pints, all donated for our cause, the construction of a bijoux theatre for the Richmond Shakespeare Society.

Dressed in our mantle of ribbons, we bang at the entrance to pubs demanding to be let in.

> *'I am King George of England*
> *Most know me as a saint*
> *And with my skill at weaponry,*
> *I make the ladies faint.'*

We perform age-old stories of St. George and the dragon. I add a pantomime horse, as well, who would take off straight for the bar, and put his nose in someone's ale, and drink to the lees while a woman, handpicked from my theatre buddies, jerks out King George's codpiece, all of course in the Christmas spirit of goodwill.

Fun for all, except poor King George who is left nursing his goolies.

As a by-product of my antics, I get a call to submit my C.V. for consideration as a Conservative candidate for the coming general election. What made the mark? Was it the old bag at the bench, King George or the horse? I'll lay my bet on the horse. It's horses that win races. Still good to be noticed, to take that leap from porn to politics. Maybe, they are the same.

1983

Thoughts from the Hustings

I end up as first Indian woman to fight a General Election for the Conservative party in the Ladywood constituency right in the heart of, Birmingham, aptly called the Bull Ring. I shall step boldly inside with my red *dupatta* waving. I'm no freaking-out lady of Ladywood. Why Conservatives is the moot question? Because Maggie runs the country and I admire strong women who can control better than me. She'll get my vote and those of all that that I can muster. I also have another good reason for supporting her that has nothing to do with politics. I shall do it for the sake of Father whose final years were torn apart by the rising of trade unions, whose raison d'etre is nothing short of being adversaries of anyone in management.

Now here was a man who nurtured his staff whom he treated as family. He went well beyond his duty of care: he shelled out for the marriage of their daughters;

he set up an annual football trophy for their children in school, and for their families, he donated a mango grove by the river that they could enjoy over the years to come.

Despite the benevolence, the rising trade union recruited his own staff to take up arms against the company. There is no doubt in my mind that its unyielding insurrection brought him down. It is responsible for the two heart attacks that finished him off. When I visited him in hospital covered in pipes and needles, he told the doctors to release him because he was a man of the field, but it was a field that was mown and harvested by Arthur Scargill and his bunch. Maggie will take on the unions, and I'll will accept the challenge on offer. I refuse to be token Tory candidate. Apart from the personal imperative, I can support the ethnic community as an M.P. Therefore, as I feel I am a worthy candidate *per se*; my academic credentials and social profile would also be compatible with the traditional image of the posh Tory, though my heart will always remain *junglee*.

Have I gone bananas? Certainly, the media has. Thatcher was hardly the flavour of the day. I was hounded by journalists and television crew. Success or notoriety?

My youngest daughter, Bem had collected a basketful of eggs to hurl at Thatcher who was on her way to Cambridge when word reaches her about her mother. Embarrassed, she turns back; felt she couldn't cast the first egg.

*

General election, Thursday June 9th 1983
Ladywood, Birmingham

Birmingham is feverish; two of my children infected! Anju, leaps forward when she sees the opposition van approaching, flanked by chanting supporters, largely Indian. Something snaps within; she steps onto the road, shouting, 'Commie!

Instantly, the van starts to accelerate towards her. She has to leap back to the pavement to avoid getting knocked over.

High drama for Arjun as well.

'Sonny, if you turn up near this polling booth next Thursday, you're a dead duck!'

I think they are getting their ducks wrong. I'm still swimming.

I get in touch with the Attorney General, and request surveillance for my children. He professes he would investigate, and improve law and order… next election! A Hamlet in Westminster!

The run up to the polling day is even worse. I am standing on an open lorry in in Indian dress with a microphone in my hand; easy target.

Suddenly, a stone is thrown violently at me, touching my hair. I can feel its *whoosh*. Had it been any closer, duck for dinner. I'm in the midst of a fairground of hate.

This violence is not unexpected. Ladywood is replete with high-rise, run-down flats filled with unemployed, Brummies. Asking for their vote is traumatic. One man sets his dog on me! Have you seen my racing sandals? They will tell their own story.

As Ladywood is a heavily multi-ethnic community, I had thought that might well be the reason why I was selected. As I'm Punjabi, that could be an added bonus. The heart land of the city contains several Sikh Temples. They seem a proud race who feel that one day Birmingham would belong to them, and more and more of their people would spread across their land. It's a bit scary when their leader orders their menfolk to be alongside me and at all times. I cannot be side-tracked by any racial confrontation. I will not be associated with just one group. I take a chance and spread myself around.

And come up with surprises.

Ladywood constituency is right in the heart of Birmingham. All-round, one can see the wealth of impact of the Cadbury family who are Quakers. Amazing to discover it is inhabited by prostitutes every night. Had I not been familiar with Bill's voyeur trips to Grant Road in Bombay, I would have done a double take at this extraordinary sight, but this time I plan to meet them.

On my way back to the YWCA, where I have stationed myself for reasons of safety, I usually pull in by the relevant curb and get to know their problems. They know that I'm called Prami and most of their complaints concern local residents and the police. I can see the argument on both sides. It seems the police would move them on, but all they can do is to shift to another road, where the same trouble starts again! It's like the monkeys in the farm house; as the *malis* pop crackers; they leap away with alacrity but sneak back when the coast is clear.

I can do nothing for the oldest profession, but they gather round nevertheless. No politician has taken trouble to talk to them before, and I got my votes. As a teacher I got them to open up about their children and the problems of raising a family given their working hours. I suggested the meer cat model that I had seen David Attenborough describe. One stands watch over children while others forage for clients. One space, two jobs.

Back in India, Prime Minister Indira Gandhi is facing trouble with the Sikhs in Punjab who demand their own separate state. Although now fully resident in England my Sikhs have left their hearts in Punjab. They now want to give voice to their giant diaspora, and force her not to meddle in Sikh affairs. Coach after coach sets off for Hyde Park, where they plan a gathering of more than thirty-five thousand Sikhs. The leader asks me to take part from the rostrum. I'm caught between a rock and a hard place. I'm here to see to Thatcher's needs, not slope off on vagrant diversions. Yet, these are the very people who have once been my people; I'm Punjabi by birth. How can grass be greener somewhere else in Delhi?

Nevertheless, I'll have a go although I have never spoken to such a huge gathering before; and my Punjabi is pathetic! But come the time, the performer in me emerges! What an experience! Loudspeaker behind loudspeaker relays my voice over an ocean of faces. At last, I'm back in track to Everest with my own private army.

Finally, I gain access to Pakistani households of Mirpur in the Himalayas, a sanctuary where no candidate had previously entered. But I knowing Urdu, and being a female, was able to do a little job for their pubescent

daughters, who have to be returned home because school uniform, even trousers, is most revealing of shape. Elementary, my dear Maggie. I now have connections. I could get the council to not force girls to tuck blouses into trousers, but to allow them to hang out and help to conceal their bottoms. A discreet alteration, but a deft solution.

As for the leafy suburbs, the twin set and pearls are already recruited. A shared tipple of sherry will do the job!

Thatcher won this election with a thumping majority, and I doubled the Conservative vote.

There is a spring in my step. I have rung another bell. Summers in the air, Aunty Glad's lambs are frolicking, but the Universe provides a woman for whom the bell tinkles before it tolls? Bill is filing for divorce and a divorced woman is *persona non grata* in our society.

1983

Richmond: The Ship Sinks

I return home, tired after a day's teaching. I open the front door with relief; time for tea. The election has drained me.

Pause awhile; there is something strange. I step straight into darkness, with just me on a bare carpet. Just a little light found its way through the half-glazed window. Everything else has found its way out.

All the pictures, paintings and memorabilia of a family growing up have vanished as if a magician had swayed a vast red shawl with a sleight of hand that made twenty years vanish with a swish. Where's the second hand brown upholstered furniture that we bought from a charity shop; where's my Father's Santhal painting of a bullock cart that he gifted me to remember our Mosaboni. Even the higgledy-piggledy assortment of cutlery has been emptied from the kitchen drawer making sure there will be no meals from tomorrow. Only the whiff of chemicals lingers. For the first time, the house looks clean as if ready for disposal, perhaps even of me. All that is left is toxic air. I see myself wearing a placard, '*Please look after this bear.*' Even though she's not Paddington, but Prami. I'm cuddle-hungry for folk to hug me. Our marriage might have headed for a silver anniversary in just a few months' time. I had this crazy notion that we would take a holiday together to cruise the Norwegian fiords, remembering a once-ago ship's cabin, but this time sans any child; a crazy old couple going wild. Now there is this nothingness of space, grief in heart, vacuum in mind, and streaming eyes making me blind. I paid for my folly with the currency of tears.

They say the *Titanic* went down quickly when knocked by the iceberg, but my ship reached the sea bed much slower. Divorce papers were quickly processed, but the struggle in dividing our assets took a lot longer; you could have pulled me through a wringer. It took away my health, my job and any belief in myself, just despondency, deep dark and bottomless. I had started to wonder whether Bill had planned this all along while his naïve wife was trying to fix the marriage with a fling on a dinghy. What it did turn out to be the reverse; it opened Nalda Club skirmishes into open warfare. In any battle there have to be winners and losers.

Eventually, Bill has to pay half of what he received from the sale of our house. Bill's' riposte: he slams a restraining order on me from entering his house. We have done our best and worst and parted for good. It will be strange living alone. When I turn on the kettle, I still make tea for two.

1983

Wales: Rite of Passage

'In all our searching, the only thing we've found that makes the emptiness bearable is each other.' Now, there's no 'other'.
Carl Sagan: *Contact*

Yes, there is another! My aunty Herbert in Wales. She has told me her door will always be open. She will be my sanctuary. Age cannot not wither her and aunty will remain forever Welsh. Their cottage is called, '*theek hai,*' that in Hindi means, 'all's well', a name the poor lady can never pronounce. Yes, all will be well in her home.

When I arrive unannounced, Aunty took one look at my face, said little but just that little, spoke volumes.

'I think you're coughing, dear child. Come inside and take a rest. We'll talk later.'

I lingered awhile as the nightingale trilled her bedtime song. A stone wall at the side reveals a shepherd who has been herding his flock with a silent a black and white border collie at rest by his feet. It's *theek hai here,* a place to wind down.

In the gathering gloom of this long summer's day, I hear a flutter behind the ivy. Carefully separating the strands of knotted leaves, I discover a trapped bird, some sort of greyish seagull struggling in panic; she's held tight within the ivy. My heart goes out to this quivering little creature and I extract her gently from her bonds. In an emotional moment she becomes me. and I tighten my grip causing her to drop off my hand.

Just then Uncle Herbert emerges from within. One look at me, one at the bird, and he goes straight to the bird saying,

'Aunty is in the kitchen.'

He steps into his adjacent garage and brings out a shoebox and pokes little holes at the top and gently lowers the bird. Business finished; he now smiles at me. I haven't left gazing transfixed at the tragedy.

'We'd better take it to the RSPCA in the morning for a proper check-up,' and adds,

'I told you. Aunty is in the kitchen.'

He didn't want any maudlin response. When I enter their cottage, it's just what I expect, not so different from the Mosaboni bungalow, but more rustic. On the Welsh dresser, rows and rows of painted plates are positioned in a rigid line: Victorian girls in bonnets by streams, by flower beds with watering cans; waterfalls cascading over rocks; a child in a pinafore swinging under a tree, and on the seats, embroidered cushions, and a framed picture on the wall with nothing but a series of embroidered stiches, her childhood compacted in Victorian sampler! And centre over the fireplace, a photograph of Margaret. She has made her home in Canada and doesn't wish to come back. I know the pain she feels. Instead of tea for two, she makes loaves for many.

A familiar odour emerges from the kitchen; 'Ah! She's baking as usual.' With dough over her hand and a questioning look on her face, she embraces me; I fill her in on my shotgun marriage. She listens without a word, yet there is a question that bothers her,.

'What did dear Mrs Lal say, pet?'

'She will not speak to me.'

There was a silence of togetherness, woman with woman. I haven't yet told her the worst part, the abandonment by my husband, the loss, the emptiness. I stumble through the words and break down.

'Everything is empty in my life; I have nowhere to go.'

'You can rely on us, child, Bertie will find you the finest egg every morning.'

I'm not a lover of cooked breakfasts, but regular eggs are as good as a permanent invitation.

The Herberts have stepped down in life and it's not Bethany the cow that causes worry, but denizens of the chicken coop who misbehave, not laying in time for breakfast.

'Have a good lie in, child; we have breakfast late', she said. 'Habit from the old days. Now we don't even have to do that! Breakfast on time.' Uncle Herbert has come in. He takes pride his inventiveness in getting lights to come on earlier, misleading the chooks that it's daylight and to get on with their clucking and laying.' Aunty giggles in conspiracy. So much colour in her cheeks; perhaps it's happiness.

*

Next morning, I find myself outside the RSPCA office, relieved that the bird has survived. There is a gathering of trippers outside.

When the officer is ready, gingerly, I present the box.

'I found this poor seagull yesterday evening in the ivy. Can I save it?'

The officer takes a quick look in the box and addresses me as an ignorant outsider.

'The bird is perfectly fine' he reassures. 'They sometimes get swept too far inland when they come to our shores to breed and in order to get things straight, it's not a seagull, it's a petrel and secondly, it's not injured as I said. That's the way shearwaters are built. Your little fella must have got blown in with the wind, and if it helps in any way to steady your nerves, put it in your head that shearwaters are sturdy birds. Hurl it out into the sea as it starts to get a little dark.'

'Murder most foul' I mutter, clutching the bird as one would a child. 'All I wanted was to save the bird.' The man is irritated now.

'That's exactly what I'm doing! Wait till the evening, hold the bird right over your head and hurl it straight out into the sea. You can't go wrong. Now, if you don't mind, Mrs...?'

'Le Hunte.' The name almost falters in my tongue.
'Mrs Le Hunte, for God's sake send the bird home!'

*

It's evening; the cliff tops are lit by mackerel skies and nesting birds fill the air with a cacophony of calls and shrieks. Portentous it is when time and space meet as one. As the light fails and the breeze picks up, the airscape is ready. There is a sense of destiny, the Herberts and I tramp along the high coastal footpath to a jutting promontory that is to be the launching site. Nobody has spoken as we climb. What was a vault will soon to be without doors as l perform a rite of passage; a goodbye to my marriage.

Watched by the Herberts, I raise my arms and filling my breath, hurl the bird into an opening space. Just when I think the poor creature will fall headlong onto a rock, a current comes its way, and gathers it like a mother. The shearwater rises in a high triumphant arc, and long wings stretched out is carried into the sea. In the air she might have seemed ungainly with stiff wings, but the moment she reaches the waves she glides wave upon them with a skater's grace.

And so, to sea, to a new beginning that, for the present moment, must command her back to the granite escarpment to find her young and raise a future.

Aunty Herbert puts her arm gently round my shoulder.
'Stay here quietly by yourself, dearest Prami, Bertie and I shall come later to fetch you.'

The Trial

Now I'm sitting on a stone on the beach below, chin resting on one hand like a Rodin sculpture and wishing I could take off with the disappearing shearwater.

'O William, William, wherefore art thou William?'

Why couldn't you simply be Bill? The man in the grey suit who left Sheen Park is William, but the man I loved naked is called Bill. Has something always been rotten in our marriage? Who's to blame? I cannot rest till I put this marriage on trial.

I shall be Crown Prosecutor, Defendant and Judge

'So, you consider your marriage a failure?'
It's a misnomer to call our coupling a marriage, your Honour; it's a mere connection of a couple of Lego bricks put together by a child.

'Surely, you were not a child at the time? Why did you choose to play a game with your life?'
'I was in a rush to escape from Mother who was planning an arranged marriage. Any Lego will do.'

'So, you left it to chance. This random Lego you've brought on trial. Was he good enough for marriage?'
He was not random, he was introduced.'

'That's no different from what happens in an arranged marriage.'
'Very different. I was in control. Shakespeare had opened the door. I could do what I wanted, *As you like it,* was my set text in school. And Rosalind was more than a protagonist; she was my heroine.

> *Make the doors upon a woman's*
> *wit and it will out at the casement; shut that and 'twill*
> *out at the key-hole; stop that, 'twill fly*
> *the smoke out at the chimney.*

'I felt empowered. I'm a strong person, I even used a bold and brash pansy behind my ear as lure.'

'So, you regard a garden plant as lure?'
'Pansies have 'come hither' faces. From their periscopic position they signal that I am available.

'So, you want the world to know, you are public property?'
'Only the man I have chosen.

'So, you think pansies have flower power to fetch him?'
'He was showing no interest and I was desperate to escape.'

'Is escape any justification for marriage?'
I must come out with truth. I cannot shield Bill.
'No, your Honour, I did not want marriage. It was the baby'.

'What baby dammit? You are speaking in riddles.'
'If there's a baby, it's no accident, Bill deliberately didn't withdraw in time. Withdrawal is the only birth control he used. When Bill found the time was right, he pushed a bun into the oven. Bill has a case to answer. Bill is the rabid dog who has to take the blame for the baby, I'm simply the bitch who surrendered.

'Are you a bitch?'
'That's not fair, I did anything and everything to please him, yet you cast doubt on my morality? All I can say in my defence is that I'm not as strong as I thought; I got taken in by his amorous advances, he had said.
I was trying to please you, I know you like a primitive fuck in the open, so, that's why I brought you here. Lots of sea and the mating cries of the gulls Does it matter if the English Channel is nearby? A mere detail; it can keep a neighbourly eye on us, or even give us a wink.'
I thought he loved me.

'But, did you love him?
'Love is a precinct of poets. I was brought up in arranged marriage culture with no emphasis on Love.'

'You have dodged the question. Did you love the man you married despite his motives on the beach?'
'The children adore him. He's the hero, I'm Fatty.'

'So, it's just the children who adore him?'
'He was a loving father.

'Perhaps, you admired him for his wit. But, did you love him? I am asking this question again and you wriggle away.'
'I can't answer it; I don't know myself. I was taken like a lamb to slaughter.'

'That's a cop out. You're' not a simpleton, I remember you clearly at the Girton Ball. Your buzzing hormones just couldn't wait.'
'Nothing happened then, just a naughty girl at naughty work; I just felt alive at the thought.'

'Did you remain alive?'
'Of course, always alive in bed till things went wrong later on. We were wrongly matched. The Queen of Hearts married a Jack of Spades. The difference mattered.'

'So, you felt superior to him?'
'Not at all! He won an exhibition in English while I struggled to reach Girton. We were two colours in one pack of cards. But of different status. That's society for you. It didn't matter to me, but my father dared not expose Bill to his world as the son of a bank clerk. He took over our lives once we reached India.

'So, you blame your father?'
He tempted us to make our home in India. It suited him. Bill changed in India.

'So, you blame India?'
'I remembered the case of Biondini. Barbil must have been a culture shock. Eventually, he reverted to spending time with his western friends. I was out of place in his life.'. I genuinely felt that Bill was ready to return home.

'Did you discuss it?'
'No.'

'Why not?'
'If ever there is a dilemma in life, it was this: I would be challenging the sixties, with a culture of undigested freedom.'

'Didn't you find it ironic, that you demanded freedom for yourself, yet hesitated to accept it in others?'
I'm already making holes in my defence. England was fast becoming a culture that is alien to me. I remembered Father's warning.

'I'm Indian, embedded in my roots. Licentious life is alien to me.'

'Yet, you, the Captain of Dramatics superseded your culture with an unwinding sari! Nothing to do with the pull of the sixties; it was the pull of the bed. Which one of you is the rabid partner?'
'I accept, bed is the cause, your Honour but Bill is not rabid by nature. I blame Bill's mounting collection of hard pornography. Arjun has started hiding them some under his pillow. He's under twelve! William DB's,

dirty books as they are called by the children, had to be dumped before Mother arrived, lest the dust men discover their contents.

'How can some shoddy books cause so much harm? Your husband is a grown man. It's a strong accusation without evidence. All I've heard is a barrage against him and he's not here to defend himself.' You never blame yourself.'
'I shall do it on his behalf. Bill was my stay for almost twenty-five years. Importantly, he gave me leeway to reach out for Everest. In no way did he try to get in my way.
Prance when you like, play politics if you wish. Why not give my salaam to Thatcher?

Bill even accompanied me on my selection interview for Ladywood. When asked whether he would support me, he provided them an enigmatic, gentlemanly lie, saying 'I do.' Two words that cleared the way for my selection.

I probably deserved defeat by making a computer game of our relationship. I had planned revenge for the years he had put me down. Bill would have to play second fiddle in the background for as a journalist for Femina, I was wooed by the glitterati and Bill was left in the scrum with waiters coming in and out of the kitchen with champagne on trays. Like Oliver Twist he had to ask for more as they tended to pass him by unnoticed. I got my sweet revenge. To that extent, I'm guilty of being scheming wife and a foolish one in taking pleasure in such small things.

Bill is a family man, calling him a Pied Piper is a compliment in these days of family break- ups. He's not ambitious like me yet never complained about my extra-curricular interests although they must have increased his domestic responsibility.

It was he who did the family shopping every Saturday and took the children with him all the way to Bristol to mow his mother's lawn. I kept gaining heights and Bill was content with his undemanding job that that allowed light relief at the pub. Then who am I to complain. I too am a party girl.

'I accept that he is a family man but that's even less reason to leave you.'

Although my case is likely to be dismissed, I'll answer your question that I have avoided so far. You asked me repeatedly, '*Do you love Bill?*' Truthful answer: I love the singer, not the song. Bill is a decent man. It was the contents of the books that corrupted him. Many pages that perused frequently, dropped open by themselves. Bill gets pleasure from sodomy, it's a painful sport for me. Our marriage ended with a scream. How can I provide evidence of this in court?

'You have admitted your failed marriage had little to do with the beach or the permissive sixties. You just couldn't grow up with the times. Harking back to Shakespeare is the worst cop-out of your intellect. Today's Rosalind might well wear jeans, and so she did in the play. Your father is no longer alive to question,

you say your children have dispersed. In my summing up, it's the books that have emerged as the guilty party. and you've thrown them away. Without evidence, all the rest is tittle-tattle. Bill has no case to answer. You have scored an own goal. I rule for the defendant.'

The judgement is correct as far as the law goes, but Justice is shown as blind. How clearly can a blind woman see?

It is the bed; it is the cause, my soul. Bill didn't leave me, I left Bill long before he disappeared. This little piggy had built her house on a bed; the mortgage was paid by sex, but the mattress wore thin over the years. When alive we surged like the incoming tide but detumescence set in soon after. Mine became the life of the sea weed waiting for the joys of yesterday for tomorrow will never come. Why not live for today?

> *'In my next life I want to live backwards.*
> *Start out dead and finish off as an orgasm.'*
> Woody Allen on Twitter

1984-2000

Towards the Millennium

'She was free in her wildness.
She was a wanderess, a drop of free water.
She belonged to no man and to no city.'
Roman Payne, *The Wanderess*

Now that I have cleared myself from bed bugs, you can find me anywhere from now. Where the wind blows there fly I; where the oceans roll, there cruise I. I'm a born-again Moulin Rouge with kisses to plunder. I may be shivering by the icy waters of Antarctica where the ship halts by an iceberg; cooling off in the Bahamas with banarama cocktails; round New Zealand with its volcanos; 'voodooing' in Haiti, kissing dolphins in Australian beeches, and if you look harder for culture, a Prami peeking at Picasso in St. Petersburg. As for zebras, they cover the savannah like the vast population in India.

Mayhap, I shall also shake hands with a rampant tiger, in the new millennium, or I shall become the flying woman whose ship will never land.

But, why Prami do you create this crazy mental map? It's folly to think one can be airborne forever. The glaciers are melting, the zebras are thinning, the volcanos are now man-made. Even the shearwater has to return home. But where is home?

Home is family.

1973-2005

Harrow:
Hopes and Heartaches
in Harrow

It was on my 50th birthday that I found a Hansel and Gretel gingerbread house as far away from Richmond as possible, a place cleansed of dark memories no longer carrying its baggage of pain.

It's in Harrow near The North London Collegiate School where I worked for thirteen years. It's not a figment of my imagination; this time my new house looks as if made of coffee and cream, inviting a lick, and I've made it eccentric just like me. I got Anju's husband, Lawrence' to model the kitchen resembling the Tropical House in Kew Gardens; there are even bananas above the radiator and a little fountain trickles water over tiny pots of fresh herbs. On the terrace outside another fountain with a stone Victoria lily has pads giant enough to float even me into the future.

Taking planning to extremes, I buy a Cambodian oxcart at an Earls Court Exhibition, where the main body of the roughhewn cart makes an impressive roughhewn table with its original holes and ridges. Good place to remind me of the bullock carts that carried Father's timber.

I was able to wipe out the past.

A little wren, makes her nest among the creepers covering an adjoining wooden shed. A robin follows me every evening as I work the earth while a male blackbird sings its dusk-time song.

On a cold winter's day, I brought home a chihuahua pup; so, minute that he fitted easily into the palm of my hand; he's a black and tan wonder with large liquid eyes and a deep black nose When I met him first, he was doing his best to fend off his larger brother. In my condition, he was just the right man for the job. As I cuddled him on the way home the winter's day turned to warmth, and a few hours later my solitary dwelling became a home.

Muffin wove a spell of magic from the moment he arrived. The doorbell started to ring. Little neighbours appeared on the scene, and in no time at all Puff-Puff had a fan club.

Like any proud mum, I told them all the things that Muffy had done. that day. We celebrated many 'firsts.' Then, there was the first walk on the lead; the Pied Piper could not have done better. My family grew with the addition of a white son-in-law presented by the children to remind me of Flash. Bon-Bon was truly a rogue addition who grew larger than the rest and took over the role of Genghis Khan from Muffin. Fortunately, the tiny. prettiest little chihuahua caught my eye.

She became girl bride of Muffin. Dearest Rani blessed my home with a shower of little chihuahuas special among them was Munni, the tiniest who was born on my pillow and in my heart. She was the first to leave me, but even today she remains next to my bed.

Behold the Barking Club of Harrow in the home of a woman totally against arranged marriage!

The chihuahuas played in the long back garden that I had landscaped with cricket in mind. It was first by the fountain, then a long oval in the middle with flowering

borders on each side for spectator and finally a spinney with a little wilderness of bluebells, cemetery for two newborns. Behind its trees that overlooked the park Father used to exercise with his walking stick. Dear God, don't I miss him. Little memories bring back a smile; he mixed up Chaucer with 'schnauzer,' a dog. Wouldn't chance him with 'chihuahua!

Whenever he wrote to Mother, he always started with, 'sweetheart', no dictionary needed for love. I'm getting sentimental with age.

Even my children appeared after the divorce, bringing Act II of the play I started with a single woman on the helm. No need to command and control now. The children are at the stage of their lives when relationships are either developing or fracturing. I was around to provide a broad shoulder. I'm glad they all remained neutral in the long day's night of the divorce.

Surprisingly, even Mother turned up. Not the marching matron of Mosaboni, nor the chatelaine of Calcutta, but still a proud widow who disdains to use a stick. I have installed a stair lift for her, and she travels up and down in her sari with the poise of a Queen, but to be honest, it goes aflutter when greeted by a carpet of waggy tails.

Although eighty-five, she still has the courage to travel on her own. She was never to come back again.

5th May 2005

Delhi: My Mother has Roots and Wings.

A legend is departing; Mother is now bedridden after a fall. I must leave my house and set off to Delhi taking with me all my now elderly chihuahuas and allow them to spend their last days still beside me.

When I saw her off at Heathrow, she told me with certitude that she'll never come back to England again. Something within her must have brought out this strange remark; perhaps the shadow of the Grim Reaper that only she can see. What I notice even now, she's beautiful. With strong, classical square jaw bone, the contours of her face can never change. But surely, I can change, be gentler and kinder in her last years and reign in the fury.

Chapter after chapter you might have noticed, I've locked horns with you, Mother. You were the darkness in my life that was turning edgy with strife. What a misfortune, I used to say to myself, to have Hitler for a mother!

'Hari ayah, fetch the brush,' you commanded; the back of the brush clubbed my burning skin. Physical pain matters not, the thrust to the soul is deadly. Even at college there was public humiliation.

When I was a student in St. Bede's, you demanded I be given extra fruit for breakfast, to make up, I suppose, for the grapes you could longer peel for your baby. After all, it was your duty to be a proper mother, and you performed it in style. I remember the slow clapping as the extra apple approached on a tray.

'Behold the Captain of Dramatics being nourished.' I wish you were there to take the curtain call.

*

When I arrive at the hospital and see her lying prone in bed, I'm forced to halt and stare in disbelief. How has the Mighty fallen! The tigress has lost all her teeth, except a single one at the top, yet she's not pitiable; in fact, her prima-donna stance is still clearly up front. She pushes away the plate placed in front of her; she will not eat hospital food. In desperation, I seek permission to bring in food from home which is normally never allowed. Even then, the egg turns out to be a problem, for how can it remain half boiled in transport!

Whosoever cooks for her is destined for a firing squad. A half-boiled egg has to be just so! For goodness' sake where in the continuum of sogginess does this quality control slot in? It was the same in Mosaboni where she ruled at the head of table, one foot resting on the dining chair, curled like a Moghul princess on a silken cushion, pronouncing her judgment to a confused cook.

Eventually, when she returns home, Mother cantankerously refuses all food, maintaining she's unable to swallow. Ignoring her, I carefully feed a beaten half boiled egg drop by drop into her mouth, rather like the way I had seen nurses feed my premature twins. The circularity of life!

Taking care of my mother for five years, I see her through her ninetieth birthday when I bring in a young pundit dressed in a pure white dhoti with a *tilak* on his forehead rather like Shyama He sits down by her bed side and starts chanting specially selected Sanskrit mantras that resonate the room; she appears asleep, but when he finishes, Mother slowly opens her eyes and folds her hands to the priest. Although not a practising person, she's visibly moved. I place a handful of marigolds at her feet. It feels uplifting and heart rending at the same time. It's a homage to my mother.

Little by little the angst of my early years fades. I see her as a happy teenager playing tennis in a white sari at the Ladies Club in Nagpur. Why am I still afraid of my only remaining parent? Yes, it was fear that coloured my life. I must now learn to understand her. Her fearsome image goes back a long time, right into her youth.

When Chand, that's her name, leaves home after marriage, her younger brother exults,

'Now the tiger's gone, the goats can play!'

He's too immature to understand the hairbrush that

blooded his siblings, created that magnificent feline specimen, all guts, no mercy; a tiger that he fears that I fear too.

At thirteen when their mother dies, Chand is left with five little siblings. Like a commander of a battalion, this young girl must have been forced to be a general to her band of foot soldiers, for no one there to teach this erstwhile happy child the subtle details of leadership? She resorted to the hairbrush.

The moment their father returns home, the new stepmother springs to action with an arsenal of lies to punish the older boys who now offer competition, for she now has three boys of her own so, to the barracks without food for my mother's protégés and poor Chand has to fight back for their territory. In such daily encounters, a tiger is born.

I have been told by Kamla Masi that she can be mischievous. One afternoon when all the children are taking a siesta, she creeps up and applies red polka dots on each nose! She must have had a sense of fun. A mother is resurrected that I've never known.

As the end nears, her mind gets confused. She tells me that she has stopped her daily 'sponging' for today, but even as she speaks, her nurse is applying soap over her chest ridged with undulating bones; every rib sticks out. She will not allow the nurse such liberty; she pushes her hand away, a commanding general to the last.

As I was bent over her face, a bony finger brushes my hand; it's the touch of love.

They'll come to switch off her respirator tomorrow; we've agreed the time. I'm arranging to get my mother

burnt while she's still alive. But I'll remember her as she was, an aristocrat.

She gave me roots in the Indian soil, but it was her stormy nature that gave me wings to escape. I've flown everywhere because of her.

> *'Say not in grief that she is no more*
> *But say in thankfulness that she was*
> *A death is not the extinguishing of a light,*
> *But the putting out of the lamp*
> *Because the dawn has come.'*
> Rabindranath Tagore: *Say not in grief*
> (Hebrew proverb)

2005-2015

Delhi: The New India
A Farm for all Reasons

Mother passed away in 2005. For more than a quarter of a century she lived a widow. Both of my parents have gone now but I'm not deserted. Using money from the sale of her elite house by the golf course, I have moved from her exclusive residence in Delhi, to a land of cows! Cows to the right of me, cows to the left of me, cows with their noses in the garbage. I've bought a farmhouse away from city lights for as you well know, I'm a country girl. My road is rightly called Silver Oak Marg, though the trees bear no relation of the Western oak and I think of them as lofty perpendicular ferns that sway gracefully like dancers with the breeze. Balancing dangerously aloft, I can just see nests of crows who obviously prefer a room at the top. Bright, cerise and white bougainvillea climb up from beneath, some even making it to the lower branches while those below tumble out and hullabaloo over the lawn.

I can see a neglected orchard at the back, and a wannabe vegetable garden, with wild cannabis growing wild like weeds, and on the roof, rows of washing lines. When I enquire why so high, the gardener replies, 'Because of monkeys!' Well, if you choose wilderness, you must expect its fauna.

When farmhouses first appeared about seven years ago, local villagers turned highwaymen waiting in the dark to ambush cars. I was warned to be careful for this is the land of the milkman caste called Gujjars, pugnacious, aggressive folk, but I found them to be nothing like that. My neighbour is a Gujjar politician who made good by selling prime agriculture property much in demand on the borders of Delhi. Money hasn't destroyed him. He's still a down to earth man though he owns more than 200 water buffaloes that he milks by hand each morning with the help of local boys. Milking finished, he returns home to sit on the floor and say his prayers' he's a typical old fashioned cow-herd, yet his garage is full of Mercedes and BMWs! This is New India for you. A nouveaux rich Gujjar is a twenty-first century sensation.

Come local election time, I've seen his posters stuck all over my stone boundary wall as his cattle join the hustings with votes cast in cow-dung as the loudspeaker flares. My eldest grandson, Tally, has seen this circus come to town and plans a bit of action for himself: cattle rustling! He'll nick a white neighbourhood cow now hiding at the approach of the procession and ride the poor creature like a bucking bronco. I find myself echoing Hari Ayah's mantra.

'Tally, such things are not for you.' And I don't just mean some innocent cattle rustling. There's a touch of wilderness in the orchard with little cannabis plants shooting out beneath the guava trees.

I would have liked a larger choice of fruit trees but the *malis* tell me if you want mangos, you must plan them for your grandchildren to enjoy. That's certainly not my objective. At the moment, I'm occupied with matters of the moment. To keep people away from cannabis safaris, I have a guard dog, a mongrel I have number 56, for that is the address of my farm. This cute mongrel who followed me home while taking a country walk, grows up to be another Bon-Bon, wanting a go at my visitors Yet, he's a fool. The feral cats laugh at him from the boundary wall, stripy brown and cream chipmunks are too fast for him to catch, pigeons and green parrots don't care; they are happy with their feeding tray, but the wild peacocks refuse to enter my garden any more. It's a pity for it would be good to have my own peacock once more and introduce him to the cook!

Number 56 has earned honours as a canine monster; his reputation spreads around the village. Roll on inspectors, police, the lot! I'm secure.

It's a relaxed lifestyle, with an abundance of family and abundance of memories. There; even a Juliet balcony! Most important for me is wrap around verandah. Here I skipped with Onesta; Father shaved in the morning; face covered with Santa's beard and to the manor born Ashi and her Mike enjoy the finest cup of best Darjeeling tea watched by the prime canine.

During one Christmas party, my cousin Meera and I decided to take a holiday to South Africa where her husband had business interests. However, my main pull was the wildlife. Flying to Cape Town, we chose to travel the garden route and took in the shanty township of Soweto. My word, after the pristine showpiece of Cape Town, this was no was no Garden of Eden! The banishment of Apartheid was simply political spin.

Stopping by the roadside were lounging spectators with hostility showing through their eyes. I felt uncomfortable as a trespasser I and tried to enter into conversation with an elderly man about my interest in cricket, and wondered why there were so few black players in their international team. His reply was equally hostile.

'Cricket was only for the white man. They throw a football over our fence and away they go to their cricket clubs.'

Well, I'm not a white man, yet I carried his guilt. We are immune to journalist's first-hand accounts of slaughter and carnage. In fact, they come with a health warning: some people might find the scenes distressing.

How long can we look the other way? I carry no weapons but I can strike with my pen.

It's a racist war-mongering world we live in. We all have a part to play, and mine is words, and thus *The Wolf and The North Wind* was born ironically after a holiday!

Mine will be a sci-fi production. I'll send a Wolf into the sky in an air balloon that he himself has designed. The higher it rises, the bloodier it becomes and more scorched the earth below. It will be a a proverbial battle between

Good and Evil, like our *Ramayana*. Obviously, the Wolf is the Dictator and the North Wind will be his hubris. I have decided on a shaman, a witch doctor for with a hint in his costume that will bring a touch of Africa and its tribal lore. And put me back in the footsteps of Gandhiji who started his own mission in South Africa.

But why is my shaman called the North Wind? There's a reason for that for the wind comes from anywhere and goes everywhere. It's Prami's message to the world that it's their turn to hitch a ride to Everest for Prami has lost her way. I have now become a fake accompli socialite even though my hair is pepper and salt omelette, whisked and frisked like a cocktail.

I'm an experienced playwright, however, and know that drama's power comes from its immediacy with actor and audience. In this case, one must generate fear or people won't budge. I'm going for a kick in the bum, best served with a wodge of black humour.

Wolf

(Kicking one or two imaginary people lying around)

All sheep and goats, my dear boy, they're all sheep and goats. Like that doctor over there they dance to my tune. You clap once and they sing, you clap two and they dance,

(Enter shaman, dancing). You clap three and they have orders to be killed!

(Wolf stops him before he claps three)

I like life to be simple. (laughs) It's all a game, dear boy, it's all a game! The end is always the same whether they dance or not the wolf swallows them.

You see, I did not lose interest in politics after my divorce; I widened my horizon.

At the moment, however, my horizon ends at swimming pool. The authorities want it closed for a farm must function as such and not be seen as a leisure resort. My solicitor suggests that declare that it is being used for pisciculture. The *mali* throws in some live catfish from the market. We photograph the wriggling fish as evidence. Afterwards, the *malis* eat them! Ugh! Not going swimming there anymore! I used to relax there at dusk when all the staff have left and the bull frogs call from the garden and bats swoop down and skim the water in the gathering gloom.

Olivia, Arjun's daughter brings a bunch of girlies in tow. The girls lounge by the pool in shades and straw hats, reading glossy magazines as they would on a Mediterranean resort.

The boy with the knick-knack paddywhack nappy has now children of his own.

Not just Olivia, but Alexander the Great, a dab hand at cocktails, shaken, not stirred. He joins his dad in the swimming pool, both ducking their heads in the water as the bats arrive. It's six o'clock, time for cocktails!

Being the house of a teacher, my farm serves as a study centre for Anju's children, Solly and Carrie, to allow them to work undisturbed. Now, that's a no hoper with number 56 barking at every visible cat and the chipmunks playing tag among trees. At least, that bits allowed!

My place become a leisure resort for even the youngest member of the family. Kashi, Bem's son is given his first birthday party under overhanging branches in the back

lawn, its branches spreading like a roof with dangling balloons overseeing an equally colourful cake. I keep fingers crossed, hoping there are no birds above and no stalking monkeys!

Apart from family, my Indian friends come over every Christmas to feast on butterball turkey imported from France.

Parties attract police; their hand is always stretched out. You cannot live in New India with a closed fist.

Eventually, disgusted with the whole politics of the place I have decided that the emerging New India is not for me. Bem has invited me to live with her family in Sydney. It's nowhere near Everest, but could be fitted in as a hopscotching route. I think. I'll join her, but maybe after a short pit stop at a milestone. I've now finished my play.

Addendum: I took it to Edinburgh Fringe Festival where it struck a chord with the African visitors for it resounded with their history and held up a mirror to their own tragedy.

2016-17

Sydney, Australia: Over, Under and Out

Although Bem may have invited me to Australia, I'm still in England. One look at her address, 1 Glenview Road, Paddington, suggests it could just as easily be in London, or perhaps some Scottish valley where we camped. Then, why shouldn't I take the leap? If convicts can shift, why not the address? It was in Sydney that they landed and Botany Bay is not all that distant from her house. No sign of Uncle Harry's brothels though Jan her husband, tells me they have now shifted to Kings' Cross. In Paddington I see terraces with beautiful wrought iron balconies that were crafted by prisoners from the iron ballast that was filled into ships to steady them on the high seas.

Or, maybe, I have hopscotched my way back to India with a familiar large Kashmiri carpet I had shipped out from Delhi and with beautiful art deco furniture that graced my mother's drawing room and later the farm house. So, the furniture, the carpet and I have made a very long journey to get here.

Outside my bedroom, the family living room too has an Indian theme with a wall covered by a huge oil painting inspired by Hindu mythology; Jan, her husband is both an architect and an artist.

They have also introduced a bespoke hand-carved wooden kitchen imported from Delhi.

Around a long wooden table, the family gather for a taste of international cuisine for Jan is also a chef. The place buzzes with the hubbub of Bem's growing family, Tally, Rishi and Kashi. These are the young people of today who will plant their footsteps on the shifting sands of tomorrow.

I should write a play for them. For I have travelled the world and they have yet to find it. I shall write a play for them; it shall be called *'Passenger'* for are we not all passengers in life?

My heroine will be an Ago-Indian girl, of mixed race like Bem. She will face the realities of life, the indignity, the racism, even rape.

> *Wendy: I always knew, I was Anglo Indian, but I never thought it mattered.'*
> Pramila Le Hunte: *Passenger.*

She will find herself as I did.

Gandhiji will once again walk the streets of Calcutta, and feel its throbbing the pulse.

The British had a go at this country but the body fought back. The heart still beats with the rugged rhythm of life.

Ibid

Lying on my bed with continuous traffic outside, I'm still in Mosaboni. Pummelling rhythm of the night, pulsating with power. First, double drums of the Santhal tribe. Thump, thump, pause, (next drum) thump-thump-thump, (pause). The girls are dancing, breasts exposed, tightly swaddled saris, sweet *frangipani* peeps lightly from their sleek, sideswept buns. They move in an arc, arms across shoulders, ankle bells tinkling, while bare-foot males swirling with their long and round drums, rotate vigorously in the middle.

As a woman of four score years, I may be tucked away in my duvet, yet I still have licence to dream.

The green berries of the *mahua* tree have ripened, their pungent odour permeates deep within the jungle, and like the tiger's mating scent, invites the lugubrious sloth bears, snugged in their caves, to startle and attend. The approaching dawn awaits their festival! Generously scattered green *mahua* berries ferment with the rising heat, and surfeiting on a feast of liquor, the bears start to dance!

The closed morning glory looks up, and its ranging empire of purple trumpets the dawn. The revellers of the night must get into action; the girls emerge from red and yellow ochre-painted mud huts, stoop to transplant baby rice shoots into prepared paddy fields and make them alive with lime-green, sun-kissed brightness, more blazing than the blue-green grasses of England. Their feet immersed in slimy rainwater, replete with hidden leeches, they sing their *phagun*, monsoon, songs. They await each monsoon. The falling waters refresh and renew the soil.

Why keep looking back, Prami for India has moved on too. The Maoists have taken over the areas around Mosaboni where I grew up and established headquarters in hidden villages. I'm told the villagers have either joined the Maoists or the moderate ones have fled. One woman even left her three-year-old child behind, and followed the gun. My wilderness is not safe anymore. But my heart still belongs to the Santhals. In their simplicity I had found my soul. Perhaps I'm a noble savage after all, but where shall I go? To the mountains?

The sweeping Himalayas that I could see from Simla can never change, nor the village of Naddi where I took little breaks, exhausted by taking care of a dying parent. My tap water came from a glacier that seemed touch-near. The Dhaula-Dhar range shone brilliant in the darkness, if I woke early enough when the cows and buffalo were let out into the field, and dogs gathered in armies across the wheat terraces, no warfare intended, just to salute the dawn.

But the glaciers have melted and the mighty deodars have been felled.

Why do I hearken for the past and for what is not? With the cornucopia of life's blessings, I'm still not fulfilled. What more can it offer? Despite her professorship at an Australian University, Bem is still an Indophile, deeply connected to its culture and religion. She will take me to Auroville one day to get to know its founder, a French lady known as The Mother.

28th January 2016

Sydney: Forever Friends

While I gaze at the forever Moreton Bay tree from my bedroom, news comes to Bem of the death of Bill. Although, we've been apart for nigh on twenty-two years, yet you return as if it's today. After you left me, I went through almost ten years of bereavement: an unhelpful shrink, cocktail of pills washed down with alcohol. I lost my job and any wish to carry on.

Bill, your Indian summer lasted almost the whole of that time. What an unhappy marriage for you; what wonderful years to follow, 'the best years of your life', so I'm told, camping across the country with the new wife and regular visits to Turkey where both of us once travelled together. Memories, some sweet, some bitter.

On the night before you passed away, you called Bem from England telling her you are dying, probably on the same night, because night is a good time to go. It had been hard for you earlier to accept the truth, but Anju who visited you regularly, saw it on your withering face.

When you called Bem, you wanted her to know that you love her, but you fumbled with those simple three words. Too British, my dear Bill to open your heart? Bem too, affirmed with tears that she will always honour you. A heart-rending exchange between father and child.

Such a shame you could not pass the message on to all your children as well. The interface of your preferred family blocked the way for a final communion between the five of you. They could not mourn your loss, only smoulder resentment and feel betrayed, for you changed your will in the final hours; a surgical knife severed connection with your own children. A new life doesn't require the sudden death of those left behind. Isn't it ironic that although only Arjun attended your funeral, there were more of your family gathered by the Ganges round the Hindu priest who gave your soul God's benediction before the same sacred fire that once witnessed our marriage?

I got bulletins of your 'dying fall' from Anju who sat by you in hospital for the final two months; she had especially brought her children to meet you. Although you may have exchanged a few words, she feels you did not wish to connect. Your past was a sealed capsule; you had moved on to a *de facto* new family. So be it. As your cancer spreads to your stomach, and the last drops of your life ooze away without accepting food, it was the same with my mother; two contrairy people travelled to their Maker in the same carriage. Their faces stare back.

Well, a force you certainly were, my friend. Like a gust

of wind that blows a boat out to sea; you set me free from the shackles of an Indian home and got me to roam. I shall think you, not so much as a husband, but as a friend. We have walked many leagues together in a way friends should be bonded to do. Your friendship was a dream that I believed would take roots, when friend moves along with friend.

Be blessed for remaining with me, Traveller, as long as you did. As the mist swirls, its droplets get heavy, dampen my cheek and flow slowly over my neck, I'm weeping on my pillow.

> *'In the sweetness of friendship let there be laughter, and sharing of pleasures. For in the dew of little things the heart finds its morning and is refreshed.'*
> Khalil Gibran

Dawn rises in my bedroom window. The huge Moreton Bay fig tree catches the light, its mighty branches spread out with formidable power, like the eight arms of Goddess Durga ready for battle, yet her face is calm and serene. The closed morning glory opens up, and its ranging purple empire salutes a new day. I am renewed and refreshed; I have said my goodbye to Bill.

> *'He was a man, take him for all in all.
> I shall not look upon his like again.'*
> Shakespeare *Hamlet*

I too will be reborn face the rising sun with the hope of another day.

2018

Auroville

And, as an hare whom hounds and horns pursue,
Pants to the place from whence at first, she flew,
I still had hopes, my long vexations past,
Here to return–and die at home at last.
Goldsmith: *The Deserted Village*

I have arrived on the beach in Auroville. As the sun rises over the shrubby wilderness; mongoose scamper in the early light. I'm almost at the tip of India for beyond the ocean rolls on to Antarctica and beyond that to eternal space. Auroville is the City of Dawn.

It is named after Sri Aurobindo, a freedom fighter like me. Whereas he spent a lifetime time striving to liberate India, I got struck down by a slap! Hunted by the British, he found hidey-hole in a tiny French colony at the edge of the British empire where he couldn't be pursued, for

Pondicherry belonged to the French. Here he lived, here he died and became a great seer, poet and philosopher. I relate to him for he too left Calcutta and went to Cambridge and on return to his homeland, he was soon thrown into prison and put into solitary confinement. Within its bars he found freedom and his soul was liberated to fulfil his destiny.

> *There is a Power within that knows beyond*
> *Our knowings; We are greater than our thoughts;*
> *And sometimes earth unveils that vision here.*
> Sri Aurobindo: *Savitri*

I have spent a lifetime chasing chimeras. It has come to me, at last that Everest is within you. You don't need to look.

This place shall be my dugout; all its allotted nights and days, a full-juiced pumpkin ripens in its place with no wish to be taken to any ball.

But of course, if you need entertainment, you can join me at the cinema. They show great western movies in the Town Hall. It's a long journey for him to take, but John Wayne has come back into my life!

'Howdy Father!'

I've been reading Sri Aurobindo's life's work, a mighty epic, that he named *Savitri*. I'm inspired by the protagonist, Savitri; she's is a woman, a symbol and a legend; a girl who'll never give up. She's a woman like me who has loved and lost her man.

I have curated his entire epic of twelve books into an hour of mediation where we I follow Savitri's journey

SAVITRI
'A PARABLE of DAWN:
A guided meditation through the journey of Savitri
A sound-scaped adaptation of the inspiring epic of Savitri, Book VI, Canto 11

Adapted by Pramila Le Hunte; Music and sound by Lawrence Mathias
Friday 27th December, 12pm -1pm, The Jor Bagh Community Center, (near market)

through the tree clad physical world of the jungles, to the cities where we ignorami wallow in their own egos making them plunge into to a dark nether land, hissing with forked tongues. Eventually, arching upwards she reaches regions where angels sing. Savitri is an allegory of redemption. I'm Savitri.

Anyone who visits me is taken to Sadhana forest, with its semi-desert terrain scattered with poisonous purple-flowed datura bushes where the mongoose hides.

I would like the little feller to have more trees as shelter for his family. The sun burns so hot near the tropics that they can only come out at night. I approached Aviram Rozin, an Israeli Aurovillan who has resurrected acres of dusty terrain and converted it to a dense evergreen jungle I see it as the future of the mongoose families, I approached Aviram, confident we're on the same page.

'What do you need most? I want to help.'
'Water,' he replied.

'Water is not mine to give; it's the bounty of the Lord. But of silver and gold I have some.

I can give you tube wells to nourish the trees. No sooner said than done, Next monsoon little water channels crisscrossed his terrain and newly planted saplings took life. I have circled back to the jungle where I belong.

I had also asked Aviram whether there was anything else he wanted.

'*Chai* shop, a regular vegan tea teahouse for our villagers.'

He's a vegan; it's his way of saving the world. Yes, I shall build a teahouse in the name of my beloved Father from the evergreen trees that are growing.

Aviram has come back to me by mail.

> *'Dear Pramila, The Shiva Chai shop is a big success! It became the centre for the local villagers. It even manages to bring together people from different villages to sit on the same bench.*
>
> *Daily around 40 local people are coming in the mornings and in the afternoons. Many women and children are coming. They are so happy! We even saw a baby drinking the chai from his baby bottle.'*

See, maybe even an old woman can be of help; even a cup of tea will do!

I have walked through these villages where I spotted sari-clad groups sitting bang on the centre of little, dusty lanes that serve for leisure and gossip, as well as parking for two-wheelers, converting as a sporting arena for local dogs, one place for all. Functioning like a randomly constructed Meccano set balancing with goodwill; it's the theatre of life.

A blast of horns echoes the village; it's Pongal, the annual harvest festival. Band-*baja* accompanies a procession, and the air fills with Tamil songs.

Sweet memories! When the children returned from the local church choir, they came home belting out the harvest hymn.

> *We plough the fields and scatter, the good seed on the land.*
> Matthias Claudius

Beautiful children of mine, you are my talisman of Love, to be honoured as long as I live. You are the grand children of the moonbeam who cherished you as a mother, clung to you, for her own had passed away. You filled a nest for her to grow her chicks. I understood and tried to stay away, give her front stage, did not always succeed. I ask forgiveness for my harshness, for not meeting your growing needs; refusing to share my love for you with the moonbeam. We could have shone together, made new beginnings in this this Garden of Eden, all three generations. Grand children of Natraj, dance with your mother who can still tread the boards, walking stick-n-all.

I once stood on Tiger Hill in total darkness to watch the sun rise over Everest. I shivered and waited in expectation, and, then from nothingness, a little white tent suddenly caught the light; it was the first ray of the rising sun; I saw my soul lit up by God! And from that a moment I thought that I had conquered Everest! But it was only self, bluffing self, like the squirt that I was.

Gandhiji has said in prayer you speak to God, but in meditation, God speaks to you. Will he do it today?

'In the infinity of space, I looked for God's grandeur, but in the clay beneath me, I found His peace. I rose higher and higher to merge in the vastness beyond. But the dark, purple grew deeper and denser; I faltered and choked.

'Then a voice said, 'Look down to your feet, little woman. Remember, you have feet of clay.'

Surely not! This Infinite Being, my free soul, it does not have feet of clay. But then the rains came, and water poured from the heavens, and my feet softened and melted into the ground, and very soon, I wallowed in the mud.

Around me, the wet earth bubbled and gurgled, and with Infinite Love, swaddled my dwindling form in clay.

> *'For you are precious, my Child, one with all that grows and blows and protected tenderly with Love.'*

Next morning, the sun rose and the waters dried, and a little lump of clay pulsed with life anew. Now it need not wander, nor does it need to search, for already in the little drop of dew, that touched it with a kiss, the two worlds had met.'

When I open my eyes, the rising the sun heralds a new day, the sky, red, orange and purest gold. A rainbow arches the sky. From horizon to horizon, she stretches her arms like a mother, snuggling the growing world nested in her loving bosom.

I once stood on Tiger Hill in total darkness to watch the sun rise over Everest. I shivered and waited in expectation, and, then from nothingness, a little white tent suddenly caught the light; it was the first ray of the rising sun; I saw my soul lit up by God! And from that a moment I thought that I had conquered Everest! But it was only self, bluffing self, like the squirt that I was. I should have known better. Everest is within you; you reach Everest because of who you are and even my raggle-taggle army played its part in my hopscotch safari.

It exposed the world in all its filth and glory. Like Father, I'm now a woman of the field and have learnt how to make life beautiful.

Respect the man of noble races other than your own, who carries out, in a different place, a combat parallel to yours – to ours...

> *Love also the trees, the plants, the water that runs*
> *through the meadow and on to the sea without knowing*
> *where it goes; love the mountain, the desert, the forest,*
> *the immense sky, full of light or full of clouds; because*
> *all these exceed man and reveal the eternal to you.*
> Sri Aurobindo: *The Religion of the Strong.*

Up and down, forward and back, the surf plays with the sand. There are fishermen mending their nets, ready to paddle into the Bay of Bengal. Their little blue boats will soon vanish into the waves.

A fisherman is squatting on the ground for morning duties; there's no Hari Ayah to wipe his arse.

He has to do the job himself with palm leaves. Little things can accomplish a lot.

Long ago, my beloved Father too was answering the call of nature under a sal tree, when he saw a rock catching the sun. He did not throw it away like Uncle Harry; he must have risen from his arse and called out in triumph. *Dekho, Dekho!* 'Look at what I've got!' It was the highest quality iron ore peeping from the seams. It made his life and the lives of many others.

A quirky parable though it be, bear in mind, life is fuelled by gastric gas. Whatever we do comes from within. You've travelled the globe, Prami; you know the whole world is infected. Reveille your troops, get moving! You still have a job to do.

I've filled myself with hutzpah like the girl long ago who dared casting the stone at the mighty British Raj. Dare again!

> *Blow, winds, and crack your cheeks! rage! blow!*
> Shakespeare: *King Lear*

Pumpkin, get off your arse!

Acknowledgements

My thanks to Theresa Maher for being my right-hand woman all the time

Alia Sinha for her original illustrations

Nidhi Gajjar for my author photograph on my inside cover

Lawrence from Shutterstock for the photograph from Birmingham 1983

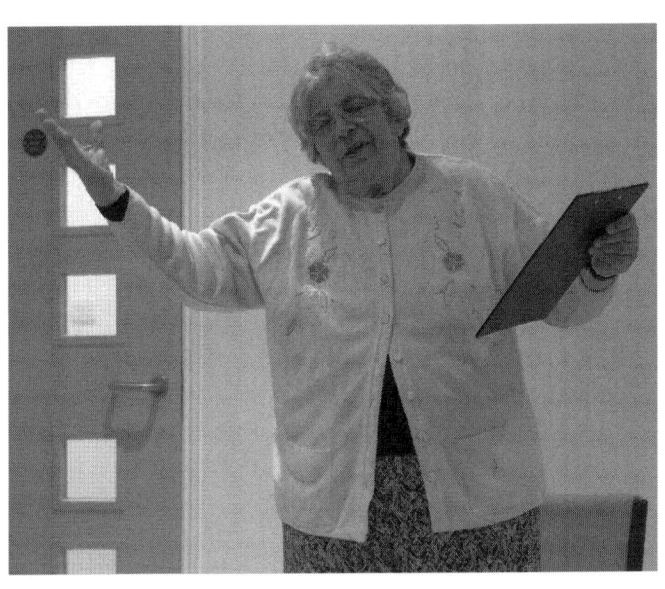